Through real and  you on a journey from becomes a guide throu and comfort. You'll tools, plus powerful wo ... and prayer to minister to all who find themselves "hopeless, brokenhearted, parched and beaten." At A Loss will end the feeling of being at a loss the next time real life happens.

Pastor Doug Webster, Author of Dear Dad, If I Could Tell You Anything

Steve Sewell understands what it looks like to be a caregiver who compassionately cares for others in a way that honors King Jesus. This book is a reflection of that passion. It is concise yet thorough, and eminently practical. If you ever find yourself serving others in a time of need, I would recommend this book as a helpful resource.

Micah Fries, Vice President of LifeWay Research

Love compelled Jesus and the results were miracles of healing. Still today, love remains the most compelling force in life. Steve's masterpiece of wisdom, At a Loss, instructs us how to love people toward healing during times of grief. His insights will always remain a treasured gem as we are called to comfort one another.

Pastor Wayne Cordeiro, Founding pastor of New Hope Christian Fellowship in Honolulu, Hawaii and author of Divine Mentor, Leading on Empty, Sifted, and his latest, Jesus Pure and Simple.

Pastor Steve was part of the care team when my own father was making his final journey home. Steve shares his stories of being with those transitioning through death, with Bible verses to help the living deal with the grief of their departure.

Roxanna Kerns, Retired Guidance Counselor

Steve Sewell has given a significant gift to the Body of Christ through the release of his book, At a Loss. This excellent resource speaks not only of spiritual insights needed to be effective caregivers, but it gives the practical tools we need to bring the light of Christ into the dark moments of people's lives. I highly respect Steve, am impacted by his heart, and appreciate learning all that I can from his example. I particularly love these words from his Introduction, "When life happens, I want to be one of those whom God uses to offer hope. I want to be one who encourages others. I want my words to count. I want my actions to matter." I believe we all echo this passion. This book will help us to make this goal a reality.

Glenn C. Burris, President of the Foursquare Church

In the 17 years we've worked with Steve Sewell, our lives have been marked by his friendship and insight into how the heart of God works in tough situations. He's stepped in during personal tragedy and given just the right thing at just the right time. We are still in ministry, due in no small part to his investment. As a new caregiver, one of our first calls was to our friend who helped us understand the importance of caring for ourselves in the journey. If any of this speaks to your heart, this book is for you.

Dr. Rod & Teresa Koop, Missionaries to Alaska (former National Director of Church Planting for the Foursquare Church)

Grief is a subject everyone experiences, not many want to talk about, and even fewer are willing to teach about. Grief is also a journey that, even with the best intentions, can be handled disastrously. At A Loss is a treasure for pastors, chaplains, counselors, and crisis teams who find themselves walking along side people who have experienced the deep pain of loss. As a Chaplain, I walk in and out of tragedy on a regular basis. It's good to know that At a Loss will be a readily accessible resource on my bookshelf.

Chaplain Jason Reynolds, Emergency Services Chaplain, Newton, KS

AT A LOSS

Learning How to Comfort Others Through the Journey of Grief Using Scripture and Prayer

Steve Sewell

Amazing Things Press

Book design by Julie L. Casey

ISBN 978-1945667695
Printed in the United States of America

For more information, visit
www.amazingthingspress.com

Dedication

It is with great honor that I dedicate this book to my father, Gene Sewell. The significance of his influence and impact in my life go way beyond the routine. He believed in me when I didn't believe in myself. He shaped my thinking about foundational areas of life, such as finances, relationships, decisions, loyalty, and dreams.

Dad grew up in Oklahoma with a very hard father, after his mother passed away while he was still very young. My father worked hard to go on his own, was married, served in the Korean War as an Army staff sergeant, and returned home to work as a barber.

While barbering was his profession for almost 50 years, he took special interest in making sure I had what I needed to be the successful person I wanted to be. He and I both worked nights while I was in junior high and high school, to save enough to put me through college. I learned a strong work ethic under my dad. In the janitorial business that we established we pushed squeegees, mops, and carpet cleaning equipment. But more important, I learned the value of hard work, the importance of enjoying the right things, and the responsibility of taking care of yourself.

My father also encouraged me to help others. He would often say to me at dinner, "What did you do today to help your peers or teachers?" He made efforts to talk to strangers and I began to do the same. He showed me how to do a "free job" (without getting paid) in the same way or better than the ones I was getting paid for, all for the sake of serving someone who needed it.

If my dad were alive today I believe he would say something like, "Good job! Now how can we get this book into the hands of people who need it?" He would then shake my hand and give me a hug. As he turned around, he might even have a tear in his eyes.

I love you Dad! Thanks for always being there for me and for teaching me to be myself and to serve others. I miss you!

Acknowledgments

I want to thank God for His provisions— ultimately modeling a care that I offer today. His love has been so kind, so rich in mercy, and expressed in so many wonderful ways. (Ephesians 2:4–7)

I am very thankful for my family. Melissa, whom I have been married to for 23 years, has been my soul mate and the love of my life. Thank you honey! My three sons Mike, Mark, and Dan...you truly are a blessing to me. The three of you are growing up to be fantastic men. Samantha, my princess, you are truly a beautiful young lady, inside and out. I praise the Lord for each of you.

I also wish to thank Ramona Hardy, my mother, who has been very supportive and helpful in many aspects of my pastoral caregiving. Thanks mom for believing in me when this was unfolding into a written package. Thank you for helping make this project happen.

Finally, I want to thank my editor for this project, who was a surprise. Trevor Behrns was a student in my youth group in the early '90s. I have stayed in touch with his family through the years and, upon visiting him recently, he shared how his blend of experiences as a pastor, editor, and designer could help a book like this come together. Thank you, Trev, for helping me share these stories from my many hours of counseling, chaplain visits, and pastoral care encounters. I praise the Lord for you, my friend! You are a great example of someone who uses his gifts for the Lord.

Contents

Introduction

I remember the time I first encountered a nursing home. I was twelve years old. I was upset that my dad was taking me away from our fun day to go there. I went with my dad (a barber) as he was going to give a long-time customer a haircut at a local "old people's home."

This convalescent home was a place of waiting, full of people who are in line to die but just not there yet. It smelled like human urine and feces. People acted strangely. There were no kids my age. No one was smiling.

I looked down one hall where a woman was yelling. In another hall, a man was trying to pull down his pants. Another set of women at a table were fighting over who was getting the last straw on the table. I watched a woman in her wheelchair hit the wall over and over until another woman (a caregiver from another room) came along to guide her through the hall, only to hear her call out an absurdity. And the only worker I saw was sitting at her station reading a magazine.

I thought to myself, "You have to pay me lot of money to do this job." I couldn't wait to get out of there.

I think I asked my dad why I couldn't just wait in the truck, about three times. He said to me, the way every dad says to their child, "Every kid

1

needs to see this kind of stuff. It will make you appreciate life more as you get older."

I didn't care about this or the old man's haircut. I just wanted to get to the Santa Cruz Boardwalk and Beach. It was Sunday. It was our fun day. He was ruining it.

I watched my dad as his insecurity rose from 0–10 in this environment. He was great with people, but even he was struggling. The smell of this place knocked you down the moment you stepped in through its big, bold doors. Dad was a barber—he could talk to anyone. But dad was at a loss for words here. He went in, gave the guy his crew cut, shook his hand, washed his own hands, looked at me to wash mine, and we were out of there in twenty-two minutes flat.

"Sometimes it takes all day to get that smell out of your nose," he said to me. I had it in mine for two days.

We all have times like this—when we are at a loss.

When your neighbor takes out the trash at the same time you go out to get your mail, and shares with you that he is getting a divorce. We don't know what to say.

When the friend who works in the bank that you have been going to for years sadly tells you that she has been reassigned to another location. We are not sure what to say.

When a couple joins you for dinner, only to reveal that her mother had just been diagnosed with a life-limiting disease and is getting worse by the day. We are at a loss for words.

This book is written to the person who takes walks, goes to the grocery store, gets gas, attends church (or not) and discovers a loss in someone else's life and therefore struggles to know what to say.

When life happens, what do we say? What do we tell the people who are in suffering scenarios? Are the all too familiar words of "I am sorry for your loss" really saying what we want to say? Or, has it become so stale that it is unheard by our grieving friends?

That's the reason why I wrote this book.

At a Loss is a book telling the stories of people who sense a feeling of abandonment as their family is ripped apart following the loss of a child, a different crisis, and other challenges.

And life happens, doesn't it?

There are moments that we encounter, big and small, that can be opportunities for awkward conversation or divine interaction. Imagine that a coworker tells you that their favorite family pastor has been re-assigned to another city across the country. What will you say to them? How will you respond?

Or, consider hearing about the failing dreams within a friend's business as the money runs out. What could you possibly say that would offer any comfort?

Or possibly, the couple in your small group that tells of their excruciating emotional pain over losing a loved one. What good can you offer?

Imagine the conversation at the water fountain at work about the heartbreak of cancer riding its wave-like pain in a close friend. What will you say to provide concern and care?

What would you tell a child when he shares with you that his favorite pet was just buried under the oak tree in his family's yard?

When words don't come easy, this book could be a helpful tool as you reach out with comfort to those on a journey of grief. This book is for the common man, woman, and teenager who is seeking to be a better friend, a better neighbor, and a better leader.

You'll see, through real-life stories, that I have been apprehended by the grace of God as a result of walking with many people through their hard times.

And it didn't happen just because I was their pastor or chaplain. A "regular Joe"—as I refer to myself—I have known God to use me in places where I had no idea there would be an incident.

My wife will even tell you that if she wants a gallon of milk she is more likely to get it herself, because she knows that I will see someone one who needs a touch of Christ in their life. They will need someone to listen and be the hands and feet of Jesus during their struggle. Most people—and this is not a slam on us—but most will keep walking; possibly even walk the other way to avoid these people, only to be shamed later within themselves because they didn't say anything. Their at a loss became their scapegoat.

Throughout these times of grief, I have been gripped with the very sense of Jesus wanting to use me—and He wants to use you, throughout this journey, to comfort those struggling with tension and heartbreak.

This book was not written for the professional, career clergy, though I have sensed that many pastors and preachers/teachers do have an ill feeling when it comes to visiting the sick in nursing homes, making hospital visits, and talking to people who have encountered bereavement of some sort. My hope is that this book could be helpful to them, too.

When life happens, I want to be one of those whom God uses to offer hope. I want to be one who encourages others. I want my words to count. I want my actions to matter.

This book is written for you so that when the people in your life are at a loss, you won't be.

PART ONE

"The Spirit of the Lord is on me, because he has anointed me to proclaim good news to the poor. He has sent me to proclaim freedom for the prisoners and recovery of sight for the blind, to set the oppressed free, to proclaim the year of the Lord's favor." Luke 4:18–19

"Behold, the former things have come to pass, now I declare new things; before they spring forth I proclaim them to you." Isaiah 42:9

Chapter 1
A New Day

My Call To Ministry

I accepted Christ as my savior when I was a freshman in high school. I was changed. At that early age, a deep call was beginning to emerge in me that I never knew before. I always thought I would be in a career helping others. Maybe it would be as a school counselor or a teacher. Perhaps I would be in human resources.

The more I prayed and sought the Lord, the more I was realizing that God was preparing me for a job that was too big for me—a career path that would be full of challenging climbs and exciting times of trusting a bigger picture—His plan for my life.

When I responded to the Lord's call on my life to ministry, I was 17. I was full of excitement and passion to help people see their full potential in a relationship with Christ.

I decided to attend Biola University in Southern California. It was here that I met some of the most amazing faculty, including the famous Ron Hafer (Student Ministries Director/Chaplain). These folks (and others) became big influencers in my life, demonstrating what it takes to be a learner and worshiper, as they modeled the love of Jesus for me. I worked hard under high academic expectations, served as a youth pastor to a group of squirrely junior high students, and fell in love with my college sweetheart, Melissa, who became my wife.

Many new adventures came along the way as I served with a dedicated heart, a can-do attitude, and a few flaws, including a severe stutter and a destructive pride. God healed my stammering speech while I was still in school, but it took longer for my pride.

As I grew in ministry I moved into a position as associate pastor, doing everything the senior pastor didn't want to do. The church soon lost its beloved pastor. In the months that followed, we processed through a search committee, hired an interim pastor, and I got the opportunity to preach on occasion.

It was during this time that I began demonstrating a deeper pride issue. Anything I didn't want to do, or tasks that were beneath me, were forbidden to rest on my shoulders. Visiting people in the hospital, attending nursing homes, and delivering bulletins and Bibles to our church shut-ins were "those people."

"Somebody else can do that," I thought. For some strange reason, it wasn't long after this time that our church received our new pastor, and an exit for the Sewell family was needed.

I began to pray, and I put out my resume and references. We kind of obliged the Lord with special requests of where we wanted to go. We heard no response. Nothing. Our interviews were fruitless. Our inquiries were useless. We waited.

After what seemed like a year, we received a call from Pastor Larry Spousta. He was the new Midwest District Supervisor of Foursquare Churches who oversaw five states, one being Nebraska. His question to me was twofold: What do you see Jesus saying to you in this season, and if you had permission from the Lord, what would you like to do for Him?

He asked me to not answer those questions, but pray and seek God for the answers and to call him the following week. It was an uncomfortable week as you might imagine. I had to confront my own pride, seek forgiveness with my wife Melissa, and consider where we would move to as our family was growing.

I placed a call to Larry and expressed myself as a rededicated follower of Christ wanting to be where God wanted us to be. I expressed my heart's desire to pastor a group of people who had been hard-pressed and who felt persecuted, crushed, and broken. I shared with Larry our desire to shepherd a church in which the congregation would be able to grow from the place they were in.

He talked to me about Nebraska and a small town there, where the church had been bruised by hurts, sorrow, and abandonment. We packed up our two kids, our dog Ginger, and all our belongings and headed east. Sight unseen, we moved into this town that we grew to love more and more.

My Wake-Up Call

So there I was, stepping out into the field of ministry as a senior pastor. It felt good. I felt ready. My family and I had arrived, moved into the parsonage and began setting up home base. As we were having dinner with our assistant pastors, Ken and Judy, I received a call from a family that I had not yet met. They were calling from the hospital and were requesting that I, the new pastor, come and visit.

The next set of words just flowed out of me. I'm not actually sure they were words; it seemed more like a thought that I had. Nonetheless, my feelings were communicated loud and clear.

"I don't do those." (Referring to making hospital visits.)

Ken looked at me. Judy looked at me. Melissa looked at me. I even think our neighbor's dog behind us looked at me. After all that hard work of letting Jesus talk to me about pride, it was coming back.

Deep down I wanted to visit but I had bigger and better things on my mind. I was interested in pastoring, but I wanted to pastor a certain group of people. I wanted "those people" (pointing to the unchurched) not "these people" (reflecting on the people who called this church their home). I was a mess.

Ken stood up, "It's okay, I'll go." He turned and invited me to come along. I reluctantly agreed.

On the way through the ER doors Ken stopped me and said, "Watch what I do."

I have never stopped observing Ken since that day. I've been watching the way he cares for people. That night Ken showed me a capacity that pastoral care givers have to offer those in need. That night was a new beginning of sorts. That night God was calling me to pastoral care.

A powerful voice of truth came through as I watched Ken interact with people in the hospital throughout that evening. He was full of compassion, an offering of open-handed love and selfless agendas. Even though he is a tall man with an intimidating stature (think Robo Cop from Nebraska), his demeanor was mild, grace-like, and full of Christ. When he held their hand, he did it with tenderness, but also with strength. When he referred to Scripture he spoke with authority but not in an over-the-top demanding way. When he prayed he was personable, relating his own feelings of bewilderment in the midst of confusing circumstances. Yet he also prayed with confidence, like he was able to see God at work no matter the situation at hand.

I silently asked God for forgiveness in my attitude and my heart, and became linked with His when it came to pastoral care concerns. I began to read more about pastoral care. I began to have breakfast at the hospital, hoping to find opportunities to give care to people who were without hope, without meaning, and moving towards their last breaths.

There are too many times to count now, the number of times I have sat with the lost, lonely, afraid, and dying, people overridden with stress and anxiety, steeped in depression, and tormented by the blows of life. God touched Ken. Ken loves God. God uses Ken to touch my life. I love God. God uses me to touch others, but only for His glory.

This book is about learning to help others through the journey of grief from a Christ-centered perspective. It's about comforting people when life happens. It's about stories of real people (names and identity have been changed) who are stricken with grief and are feeling hopeless and alone. They need someone to show them the love of Christ in word and deed. They need people to step into their lives and be a "Ken."

My desire is that you will gain a deeper sense of appreciation for people's stories as they live within their struggles. My aim is to equip you, so you are able to offer "just in time" support while knowing what to say, what to do, and how to pray. It's my hope that a little bit of Ken will come out of these pages, a little bit of me, and a whole lot of Jesus.

My relationship with Ken is strong, even to this day. The Lord used him to start a pastoral care in me that I had somehow blocked when I first became a senior leader. Today, almost 20 years later, I find myself in stores, gas stations, and coffee lines talking with people suffering in some of the worst scenarios. As I listen and engage with care offerings, I sense an overwhelming peace...the kind of peace that gives rest. I am doing what I was created for.

I want to encourage you to go out to the stores, gas stations, coffee lines, and parks in your community with ready-to-use skills. I am hopeful that when you go into your office and someone shares a hurt, a loss, or a transition of some kind that you will be ready to engage with presence and "all in" listening.

Also, that you will be slow to speak, avoiding useless, purposeless sayings that everyone else says. No more will you use the phrase, "I am sorry for your loss" without a more defining sentence or two that gives comfort. When you show up at your kids' or grandkids' soccer game and you ask how someone is doing, you will be equipped to use these skills to encourage and help them have hope for healing.

I also want to encourage you to make use of the appendix to this book, a resource of collected wisdom from years of ministry. And feel free to refer back to it often as you comfort others through the journey of grief.

The stories within the pages of this book tell about the lives behind the masks we wear when we tell people "I am fine," "I'm hanging in there," or "I don't know what to do." It is my hope that they will inspire you to action, providing comfort, hope, and love to those in need. It is my prayer that you will be propelled into a ministry of pastoral care in whatever spheres of influence God has placed you in.

Join me in prayer:

Lord, captivate my attention to be on You. Help me to see my life as hopeless, useless, and underutilized without Your touch, Your power, Your provision. Forgive me in my pride and all my ego-crazed functions. Give grace to the days where I want more of me than You. Offer your strength when I am tired and don't feel like being a good neighbor, a better friend, and a godly spouse, parent, worker, etc. I dedicate my reading of this book to You. Call unto me. I am ready to be sent!

In Jesus' name, AMEN!

"Look after each other so that not one of you will fail to find God's best blessing" Hebrews 12:15

Chapter 2
The Purpose of Comfort Care

Wherever I am asked to speak about when life happens and we find ourselves at a loss, I begin by teaching that people grieve because this world is full of heartbreak and death. The introduction of sin (as outlined in the book of Genesis 1–3, and in Romans) produced a groaning in our heart. We long for a restoration and revitalization. All of our losses and transitions are reminders of this deep grief, a continual reminder that things are not the way we want them to be.

"We know that the whole creation has been groaning as in the pains of childbirth right up to the present time. Not only so, but we ourselves, who have the first fruits of the Spirit, groan inwardly as we wait eagerly for our adoption to sonship, the redemption of our bodies. For in this hope we were saved. But hope that is seen is no hope at all. Who hopes for what they already have?" Romans 8:22-24

One of the purposes of our grief is to keep us looking towards Jesus and not relying on the satisfaction of our earthly scenarios. Our hearts naturally long for the peace and wholeness of the Garden. Yet, the burdens of this broken world weigh heavy on our hearts. We are travelers on a journey in a foreign land who have not yet arrived to our true home.

Homesick

My mother and father divorced when I was seven years old. There was a lot of heartache that year as I began a new life of living with my mom and stepfather, yet spending every other weekend and two months out of each summer with my dad. It is hard enough growing up with your parents in the same house for a seven-year-old, but double it when emotions run to extremes, each parent speaks poorly of each other in front of me, all while I'm trying to cleverly use all of this to get what I want. And, to make matters worse, my mom and stepdad chose to move from California to Albuquerque, New Mexico, a place I had never been to.

I was in torment. My friends, school, home, everything I knew about life was changing. It was going to be challenging, to say the least, to see my dad. Sure, the newness of change was encouraged by my mother, indicating that I would meet new friends, have a new school, and not have to share a room with company when they visited. She also promised that I could call dad anytime I wanted.

I recall the feelings I had when I made the decision to move from my mother and stepfather's home to live with my dad, when I was 12. I loved my mom but I also loved my dad. The older I got the more I felt awkward about the visiting, and talks on the phone. Something was telling me that I was making a decision to move. It would be one of the biggest decisions of my life.

Like it was yesterday, I remember my dad picking me up in New Mexico where my mom, stepdad, and I lived. We were going to make the trek across the highways to California where he lived, my original homeland.

I remember feeling ashamed that I was leaving mom. I can recall the nights of tears, with my stomach hurting for days on end. My heart ached. I was grieving the loss of living with my mom even though I had made the deliberate decision to move. And even though the decision was support-ed by my mom, I still felt like I was hurting. My mother even told me of the pain I might have as we discussed living with my father. But in my heart I knew that moving was the right decision.

When we arrived in California, my dad took me to the doctor to get a better understanding of my stomachache. The doctor looked at me and my dad, sat down, and said the words that I will never forget: "You are homesick." It made sense to me since I had feelings of homesickness while going to camp, while spending a week with other family members, etc. These very real physical, emotion-al, cognitive feelings were all very real.

Interesting things happened after that doctor visit. He put me on a BRAT diet (bananas, rice, applesauce, and tea), he encouraged me to call home to my mom as often I wanted, and to truly begin my new home life in California. It worked. I was healed of my homesickness because I made steps toward my new home. I began to get involved in activities. I met new friends. I got on a routine that changed my life. It worked.

Suffering is a form of homesickness. We desire to be well, in familiar environments, and for everything to work correctly. Perhaps suffering can be viewed as our longing to be with Jesus, in Heaven, which is our true home. The more we encounter Jesus, learn from the Bible as our life sourcebook, and commit our life to prayer and service to the Lord, the more we place our eyes on Jesus' plans and His place for us.

Conflicts, chaos, and confusion have a way of bringing us closer to what's really important. The struggles and sorrows of our deepest disappointments in this life cause our focus to shift. Often, loss interrupts the settled security of our lives, opening us up to receive the love of God and others in powerful ways. And ultimately, God is able to use our grief to grow us in a forward motion.

God will use the wonder of mystery and the tension of the unresolved to deepen our trust in Him. It is through our suffering that we are developed, in cooperation with the Holy Spirit, toward maturity in Christ. So, we long for our true home and hold fast to the hope of heaven as we learn to follow Jesus each step of the way.

Romans 5:1-5, "Therefore, since we have been justified through faith, we have peace with God through our Lord Jesus Christ, through whom we have gained access by faith into this grace in which we now stand. And we boast in the hope of the glory of God. Not only so, but we also glory in our sufferings, because we know that suffering produces perseverance; perseverance, character; and character, hope. And hope does not put us to shame, because God's love has been poured out into our hearts through the Holy Spirit, who has been given to us."

I have two premises to share with you as you begin this reading journey.

1. A change of heart occurs in people when they recognize that God has more for them than they had ever imagined.

Most people will go through their life with a limited vision, one that is not connected to a bigger perspective—a God perspective. When we see through the lenses of what God has for us it is much loftier, much more beautiful, and much simpler than the pictures we have put together of how we imagine life should be.

For example, I've always had a severe speech impediment. When I discovered that God was going to use my stutter for a good cause, I was astounded. My thought all along was, "I am not good at speaking. My stuttering is like a stammering train wreck."

When I came to accept Christ as my Savior and Lord, I soon discovered God was going to use me in spite of my stuttering and speech deficiency for something good and useful. God truly turns what we may see as weakness into something beautiful and useful in His eyes. (See Isaiah 61:1– 3.)

2. In Jesus' encounters in Scripture we often find His mission is to adjust people's thinking, especially as it relates to the ministry of serving others in need.

We need to understand the biblical call to serve others. When we do, we discover that through the Holy Spirit's empowerment the priorities of our lives are realigned to the values of Christ. It is the mission of God to help us see our life as a mission for His purposes. This includes comforting the grieving, encouraging the brokenhearted, setting people free who are in captivity to their sins, and building up the Kingdom of the Lord. (See Matthew 5:38–42, Luke 5:17–26, and Luke 18:15–17)

It brings me great joy to introduce to you a biblical approach to comfort care ministry. I encourage you to read God's Word through this new set of lenses. How do you see God's heart for those in need expressed in Scripture? How can you begin to see the people you encounter the way God does?

The values of providing comfort
to those who are grieving

In my experience with many denominational churches, and with those who are independent, I have come across an epidemic within the Body of Christ as it relates to people. We often think more of our buildings, programs, plans, and schemes than we do of the lives that we aim to teach. It may be one of the reasons why people in the churches don't feel loved or cared for. Perhaps it is also the reason why people are leaving churches to become more involved in other forms of communities, where they serve others rather than simply teaching the paradigms, platforms, and positions taught by the churches.

One church that I was asked to speak at invited me into their leadership team, to share a devotional and facilitate a conversation about long-range goals for their vision. A sign in the entryway was my first clue that this might be a challenge: "Wipe your feet, check your attitude, and leave your tithe as you come in." I decided to change my devotional to the story of Jesus washing the disciple's feet and a call to serve the community instead of protecting the building and its programs. No one can make this stuff up. It's happening. (By the way, the church I mentioned has since closed after accepting my long-range goal facilitation...change the way you lead or shut down.)

People are the church. People matter to God. People are used by God.

First Thessalonians 2 leads us into a number of principles for us to practice as we put into place a ministry of care. Keep in mind this is not a ministry that needs a board, a set of rules, and a financial portfolio. This is a personal model of caring for others, found in the Bible, that can also be a great model for any church that wants to serve others well. Take note of what it contains and you will be forever changed.

First Thessalonians 2 deals with the way that we ought to care for others. These should be the core values of everyone who wants to answer God's call to care for people. Notice some of these observations:

1. People of God search for people—they take initiative. In verse 1 it says that **"our coming was not in vain or a failure."** Paul had a reputation of going to people to lead them to Christ, offer compassion, and spread the Good News of Christ. His methods were strategic. He was on a mission to tell the world of what God had done in his life, and how that same God who opened his eyes could open their blind eyes too. It should not dumbfound us to realize that God uses people like us to share who He is. We just have to be willing to say, "Yes—choose me."

2. In verse 2 it says **"in spite of strong opposition."** It takes sacrifice. We have to choose to look past our own nose to see who needs love, care, and comfort. We will have to make a choice between our own desires and wants in order to help others. The church in which I received Christ as a young man invited me to participate in a servant leadership program, and they invested in my training to help me become who I am today. I would not be in ministry today if it weren't for a couple of people saying "What about that guy?" (I'm fairly certain that it cost them a little more in reputation than they might have anticipated, due to my sinful nature. I sure am glad they were willing to "pay the price.")

3. Verses 7-8 show us a picture of relational love. Read the words over in those verses and you will see words like "gentle, tenderly caring, sharing, and dear." A love beyond everything else is what is in these verses. The Bible speaks of relational love in every one of its 66 books! The world does not need a rule-driven church that sets people apart from Christ. Your community needs your church and YOU to be relationally engaged with His love. Start today by reaching out to those in your immediate circle. The call to Christ is the call to relationally serve.

4. Look at verse 9, which speaks of generosity. When we were pastoring in Nebraska, I learned of one of our neighbors down our busy street who needed a fence for her front yard. (A mother and her two kids lived there.) I remember driving by the house and waiting for someone to be home. I then called a friend and he met me in the yard to measure for a chain link fence. That following Sunday in July during our worship service I called for a special offering of $378.70, the exact amount of what was needed to put in the chain fence. I figured it would take two Sundays to gather that amount from our small church, but halfway through the service on that first Sunday one of the ushers informed me that a check had been written to cover the project. We used the additional donations from that special offering to start a generosity campaign to help those in need. A campaign to care. Out of generosity comes care.

5. The next principle is Integrity (verses 10–12). I remember my friend, Doug Webster, telling me when I was younger that integrity meant being unimpaired by the values of Christ. He knew I needed to work on this area so he broke it down to me like this: "Am I becoming more like Christ or the old Steve?" (I still like to ask that question today!) As Christians we are to be like Christ. After all, the word "Christian" means "Christ in us." What does being a Christian mean to you? If it means anything else than Christ, it may need to be adjusted.

6. Verse 13 points to another principle that is related to integrity: Truth. Over and over again you will notice that Paul did not point people to himself, the teachers of the Laws, or even traditions. His mission was to point people to the truth of the Lord Jesus Christ. I remember hearing Rick Warren, pastor of Saddleback Church in Southern California, at a conference for pastors when his popular book, Purpose Driven Church, had just been written. He said, "Our world desperately needs the truth of God. We sing 'God Bless America', 'Let Freedom Ring', and other hymns of faith and tradition. If people really meant those lyrics, we would be a different country." I challenge you to point people to Jesus as they go through suffering and grief. Dr. Phil, Dr. Oz, and Ellen DeGeneres have good shows on TV, but they can't offer the kind of comfort and peace that only Jesus offers. Jesus promises us that following his example sets us free from bondage, illicit endeavors, and chains of carelessness by others.

7. Finally in verse 14, 1 Thessalonians 2 talks about people who develop others. Similar to sacrifice, this principle deals with imitation. An old African proverb reads: "If you want to go fast, go alone. If you want to go far, take somebody with you." Perhaps we are going so fast in our lives that we miss the opportunities to serve others, to give care to our neighbors, and other chances to be a blessing.

If you were to put all these principles together you might get Rod and Teresa Koop, my good friends who now serve in Alaska as missionaries with the Foursquare Church. Their life story is etched into my life as people who continually take an interest in reaching out with grace, using a relational approach to demonstrate what true pastoral care looks like. They have stories that would make you say, "Man, I want to be around them."

The Koops care for people that everyone else looks away from. Rod and Teresa choose to make it their mission (within the vision of Christ as the backdrop) to make Christ's love the only answer for pain and suffering. I want to be around them!

Don't misunderstand the notion of Christ... He came to love the world and to lead you and me to a life of service to those who are hopeless, brokenhearted, parched, and beaten. You and I can participate in this love to the world by being a man, woman, and child of these characteristics. Stop for a moment before you continue and reflect on your own evaluation of these verses. What does Jesus speak to your heart about these principles? Reflect on these as much as you sense necessary.

"For just as the sufferings of Christ flow over into our lives, so also through Christ our comfort overflows." 2 Corinthians 1:5

Join me in prayer:

Lord Jesus, I am thankful for the times in my life when You have carried me. Thank You that Your hand has been upon me and that I am not far off from You. Thank You for the areas of my life in which I have been able to trust You fully. And I know that there have been areas and places where conflict has come and I have not allowed Your grace and truth to enter. Therefore I may have not allowed myself to trust You. I ask forgiveness in this. I want to trust You, even in my weaknesses. I want to trust You in my problems. I want to trust You in my chaos. Help me to put you first. Lord, use me when my friends are homeless, homesick, or hopeless and are at a loss. Help me to know that as I reflect on You, my grace is sufficient for me. Lord help me to model this kind of grace, this kind of love.

In Jesus' name, amen.

"I do not ask the wounded person how he feels, I myself become the wounded person." Walt Whitman (taken from "Song of Myself")

Chapter 3
Becoming Relational with Scripture and Prayer

It was during my high school and college discipleship years when I learned the fundamental value of Scripture. As a young Christian my youth pastor, Johnny, and his staff taught me to memorize the Bible verses that stood out to me during Bible studies and sermons. They modeled a "take notes" method of listening that is still with me today.

I have a great appreciation for how Scripture has changed me, my family, my friends, and my life in and out of ministry settings. I love to take notes during sermons today. It helps me stay focused and disciplines me to listen and "take in" what the message has for me.

During that same formational time in my life, I met with people who wanted to pray for me. I was astounded by the fact that people who loved me wanted the best for me, so they wanted to pray for me. I learned how to pray as a result of listening to those prayers. I believe I am a man of prayer today because of those men and women who cared enough to pray for me and with me.

One such time was by one of the elders of the church coming to visit me in my home after I came forward to affirm publicly my salvation experience during an altar call. I wanted to be baptized. As you might expect, I was excited to take this next step to follow Jesus, but a little apprehensive about some "suit" coming to my home, seeing the way I lived, and making judgment calls. I was concerned that I would not be able to meet his expectations and that he would give me a "fail" of a grade about me continuing at the church as a follower of Christ. I felt anxious.

The elder was to arrive sometime after school and before my dad was to come home in the evening. I had cleaned my room (just in case he wanted to see it), covered my posters of Farrah Fawcett and Christy Brinkley in bikinis (hey...it was the 80's and I was 16) with sheets and large towels. I borrowed my neighbor's big Bible to place on our coffee table, and I stole (yes I stole) two student Bibles from the youth room the previous Sunday morning, to place throughout the house.

I wanted to be ready, to look like I really followed Jesus. I wanted to show the elder of the church that I was a good teenager, a good candidate to be baptized. I wanted to impress this guy.

To my surprise he showed up in jeans and a t-shirt. It was one of my friend's dad's. It took the edge off, but still I wanted to impress him. My own slacks and dress shirt seemed out of place at this point, but I still rolled with the punches and welcomed him in. I turned down my church choir cassette tape of How Great Thou Art and offered him something to drink. He was on his way to his younger son's soccer game so he wanted to keep things going.

I invited him to sit down, right in front of the big Bible. He looked at it as I was trying to point him to look at it and smiled. I noticed that it read "The Catholic Family Bible and Book of Prayers."

"Oh no," I thought, "I didn't read that part!" I began to sweat. He looked away and began asking questions to get to know me.

He talked to me like I was one of his son's friends, not the way I expected. He showed me respect and common courtesy. I was taken off guard. Then he asked me if I was nervous about him coming over. I asked him if it was that obvious. He smiled and said, "Well you do look a little anxious."

I admitted that I was a wreck trying to plan for his coming. Then like every other time I am nervous, I became transparent and began to share everything. It was a disaster.

He asked me if I usually have Bibles all around my house, play church choir music on the stereo, and dress in slacks and dress shirts. He asked me if I was always this stressed. I said no.

The next words out of his mouth felt freeing, "I did not come today for you to impress me. I came to hear your story about how Jesus touched your life at Winter Camp last year. Tell me about that trip. How was the skiing? What were the kids like? How was the camp food? Tell me about what you learned from chapel sessions."

To say the least, I relaxed. I unbuttoned my collar and relaxed. The elder visiting my home became a friend coming over to get to know me, to hear my story, and to talk to me about baptism and what it meant. And the time...well it zoomed by.

On the way out, I remembered that I had his son's jacket in my room from the previous night and asked him if he would take it back for me. He must have not heard me say that I would be right back because he followed me to my room to retrieve it. Now I was embarrassed for sure. He was cool though, looked at my walls that had towels and sheets hanging down, seemingly to have things covered. He peeled back the towel to took a look at the Christy Brinkley poster, smiled, gave me "the guy nod" (the one where we know the same thing but for some reason can't say anything out loud at the moment) and broke all the rules. He quietly said to me on his way out, "She's hot...I would uncover that one."

The elder prayed for me on his way to his car.

This person shattered all my crazy ideas about when a church leader comes over and wants to talk to me. He related to me the very same way I relate to people; conversationally, open-handedly, affirming. He was cool. I thought to myself, "I could hang with this guy!"

31

Somewhere in our life, we come up with these made-up expectations that we think other people want us to have. But the way I see it, Jesus calls us to be who we are, truly who we are, so that His Word and presence can make the inner change that will make a huge and lasting difference on the outside.

That's the story of Scripture and prayer transforming me and you. And when our friends and loved ones are at a loss, we rely on how those Bible passages radically moved us forward in a like-minded way in Christ.

As simple as it is, Bible study and prayer have been my go-to sources for hope and guidance as I have entered into and out of the long hallway of grief. If I am grieving I run to the Word and call out to Jesus for strength.

During one point in my ministry I felt attacked more than I had ever felt before. I remember the moment very clearly, because when I entered the church building upon arrival it was sunny and windy out. During the time I was inside the climate had changed dramatically and so had I.

I had finished cleaning up after a meeting and headed into the sanctuary to pray to finish out my night, as I normally did. As I was praying, I began an almost marching walk and began to raise my voice calling out to the Lord for mercy, redemption in my city, and a fresh touch of the Lord in my life. I envisioned a storm of fresh "rain" upon the church, and I thanked God for whatever He would send. Just then, a huge thunderclap filled the air and what seemed like buckets of rain began to be poured out on the earth. I began to weep at what God was mightily demonstrating for me in response to my prayer. There have been many times like these where God clearly speaks to me while in prayer.

Regular prayer meetings, with Bible study, are essential to my life and ministry. They are two of the most powerful and personal points of connection we have with God, to help us grow in our faith. They point us to God's plan, His will, and His purpose for our lives. They keep us real.

The Caregivers Sourcebook

Our Bible is filled with individuals following God. From the life of Adam to the end of time, God's promise of love, acceptance, and forgiveness offered to people who needed a Savior is found in the ancient Scriptures. These same Scriptures are for us today, too.

Since becoming a Christ follower I have studied the Bible earnestly. It has become my playbook for my life. And when I don't get plugged into what it has for me, my life seems to be depleted and powerless. I grow weary when I am not tuned into the pages of the life source of the Scriptures. Consider what the following verses tell us about the value of Scripture:

"And we have the word of the prophets made more certain, and you will do well to pay attention to it, as to a light shining in a dark place, until the day dawns and the morning star rises in your hearts." 2 Peter 1:19

"The word of God is living and active. Sharper than any double-edged sword, it penetrates even to dividing the soul and spirits, joints and marrow; it judges the thoughts and attitudes of the heart." Hebrews 4:12

"Your word is a lamp to my feet and a light for my path." Psalm 119:105

"The entrance of your words gives light; it gives understanding to the simple." Psalms 119:130

"Do not let this Book of the Law depart from your mouth; meditate on it day and night, so that you may be careful to do everything written in it. Then you will be prosperous and successful." Joshua 1:8

This same Word of God that has changed your life can transform the lives of those you comfort. Each verse that is shared with those who need encouragement is refreshment. At the point of people's dead end, crossroads, or straightaway, God can use His Word to direct people to hope. And

He uses ordinary people like you and me to show the way.

Have you ever seen the famous phrase attributed to both Theodore Roosevelt and John C. Maxwell, "People don't care how much you know, until they know how much you care."

Think about that for your own life. Isn't it true? People don't care how many Bible verses you can spew out of your mouth if you don't care about their lives. Care as you share.

Prayer at Every Turning Point

One of the favorite phrases I learned from one my discipleship classes in college is from Samuel Chadwick, "The number one concern of the Devil is to keep Christians from prayer. He fears nothing from prayerless studies, prayerless work, prayerless religion. He laughs at our toil, mocks at our wisdom, but trembles when we pray."

Reaching out to God during my own turbulent times has always included prayer. God has shown Himself faithful to me when I have cried out. My tears were collected. My Savior and Lord has been a comfort. During most of my pastoring experience I cried out to God. I wondered if I was doing the right things to "grow the church." I wondered why things were not as they were in my mind. I prayed for finances daily. I prayed for peace in my family. When my all simply wasn't enough, I prayed.

And, during the good times in my life I have prayed. One of my co-workers said to me, "After something good happens, you always seem to say 'Praise the Lord.'" I took that as a compliment. I really want my whole life to be bathed in prayer, the good and the bad. Consider what the Bible reveals about prayer in these verses:

"...how gracious He will be when you cry out for help! As soon as He hears, He will answer you." Isaiah 30:19

"This is the assurance we have in approaching God: that if we ask anything according to His will, He will hear us. And if we know that He hears us—whatever we ask—we know that we have what we asked of Him." 1 John 5:14-15

"The Lord is far from the wicked but hears the prayer of the righteous." Proverbs 15:29

"Call to me and I will answer you and tell you great and unsearchable things you do not know." Jeremiah 33:3

As I comfort people in all kinds of settings—the same kinds you are in—I find it incredibly essential that I plug into the power of prayer.

May I offer you the same devotional instructions that my youth pastor Johnny gave to me: The **ACTS** of Prayer.

Adoration—Give praise to God for his love for you. Begin your prayer time with praise for the works of His loving kindness, grace in your life, mercy that has been given, etc. Let the words of your mouth give praise for who He is before you ask him for something.

Confession—Part of our understanding of who we are in Christ is that we are sinners in need of God's gift of grace. As you pray for yourself and with others, confess your own control settings and how they need to be switched over to the Lord. Ask God to cleanse unrighteousness in your life, known and deliberate to the unspoken and unaware. Understand that you don't need to be born again and again and again. Justification gives us eternal security positionally in Christ, but the presence of sin hinders our intimacy and fruitfulness. Once you have sonship you can't lose the relationship. But you can lose fellowship. This confession opens the doorway for God to heal, restore, and renew.

Thankfulness—Do you see the progression in this prayer model? Having a grateful heart is at the core. In this step I have found that I am only able to be thankful when I have seen God move in my life. I sometimes will have sessions of prayer when I simply recall the acts of God in my past and say "Thank You!" to Him. This is my favorite part of prayer, because I get to say more praise to my Savior and Lord. "The call to Christ is the call to be thankful," says Dr. Ralph Kraft, my first pastor. I still have those sermon notes. After being a Christ follower for over 32 years I still believe it.

Supplication—Our final act of prayer in this model is supplication. This word simply means requests, wants, and needs. After we have praised God, confessed our sins, and thanked Him for his grace and mercy, then we ask God to show us His power in our requests. You don't have to spend a lot of time in observation to recognize that we want to tell God what we want Him to do. While this is understandable, I wonder if we should approach things differently—starting out in praise and giving God control of our lives, then asking for Him to show up in our circumstances, reveal to us His plans, etc. So after you have praised God, go ahead and let Him know what's on your heart and what you need from Him. Go before the throne of grace and present your friends and loved ones to Him.

Join me in prayer

Dear Lord, I do not know how long this season of grief will last. But I trust you will accompany me on this unfamiliar path as you have done with those before me. Amen

Faithful, Available, Teachable

Why is prayer and personal devotional time in God's Word so important to the life of a comfort giver? Simply stated, we cannot have an eye for miracles in other people's lives unless we have experienced them ourselves. Without a vibrant devotional and prayer life, I am bankrupt. If I am going to be useful in someone else's life, I first have to be able to hear the Lord in my own life.

As the elder of the church drove away I called my friend, his son. He laughed with me as I told him what I had done, especially with the posters in my room. We talked about getting together later to work on our history class project. He said to me, "It's cool that you want to be baptized, Steve...but its *way* cooler that you are trying to live for Christ like an ordinary guy."

For the next several years as I would see the leader at church, he would always give me that same "guy nod." I saw him last year at a funeral when I was in California. I approached him and gave him and his wife a hug. He gave me the nod, and asked me if I still had that poster. We laughed. His wife gave him a puzzled look. He looked at me, looked at her, and looked at his son.

"Oh Mom," my buddy said, "You wouldn't understand."

Join me in prayer

Oh Lord, as people are reading this and wanting to be an active part of bringing comfort to others, call them to an inward look at what You want for them and how You want to serve. Call them to a closer walk with You. Shepherd them to your Word and to prayer, so that they can be filled up with you first. Direct their paths to a rich and vibrant quiet time with You. Show them that they need You. Break forth their need for Your touch of faithfulness in a regular devotional life so that they can be available and teachable—ready to be a giver of comfort and Your loving kindness. Amen

PART TWO

"Praise be to the God and Father of our Lord Jesus Christ, the Father of compassion and the God of all comfort, who comforts us in all our troubles, so that we can comfort those in any trouble with the comfort we ourselves receive from God. For just as we share abundantly in the sufferings of Christ, so also our comfort abounds through Christ." 2 Corinthians 1:3-5

What you said:

"You can always have another child."

What they heard:

"My precious child that I just lost can be replaced with another one just like it."

What you wanted them to hear:

"I've never experienced anything like this before and I don't know what to say but I want to be supportive and understanding. Can I come over to sit with you and listen? Can I pray for you? God loves you and wants to hold you close during this painful experience."

"Now, God be praised, that to believing souls gives light in darkness, comfort in despair." William Shakespeare

Chapter 4
Battling with Cancer

Olivia's Story

When Olivia was growing up she dreamed of her blonde hair up in curls on her wedding day. Actually, she had many dreams of this special day thanks to her mom and her dad raising her like the princess she was.

"She grew up strong-willed, athletic, and as gentle as a butterfly," her dad said as we talked about her life before she was diagnosed with cancer.

Olivia knew her dreams would come true. All the way through junior high and high school she was academically eligible to go anywhere she wanted to for college. However, she wanted to stay close to home to support her parents, their farm, and the small-town lifestyle she grew up to both love and hate.

Her favorite memories included learning how to swim in the lake, wrestling with her brother over who got the last piece of chicken, and how her first date was with her longtime friend who lived down the street, and who would later become her husband.

"Days grew shorter as the time passed, thanks to my illness," she said to me once.

When I asked her about the time impacting her that day, she said that between the effects of chemotherapy and her head pounding, she was doing okay. She wasn't craving anything except for the longing to be the young 20-ish something woman who had just got married.

"I don't wish this on anyone, even that girl who broke my record in making the most free throws at the local basketball shootout during halftime my senior year." She laughed—well kind of; the only kind of chuckle she was able to give was by her eyes and smile. Nothing like she could do when she was without cancer.

As I sat next to her and the hospice nurse was talking to her parents, she reached out to my hand and said, "I know what she is doing. She is preparing them for the worst."

I asked her how she felt about the worst, and her dream of living a long life with her new husband on the farm, just like she had planned. Her words shook me to the core.

She replied, "I am okay. But no parent should have to bury their children." She wiped the tear from her eyes and pushed the button for her medicine to give another dose. "This thing works great," she said to change the subject.

Olivia believed in God and consistently lived out her faith in a way that made a significant impact in the lives of others. She attended Sunday School each week and helped serve in the holiday meals (her famous chocolate chip pie made with the recipe her grandmother passed down was a favorite among the entire town). She also managed the town "Veteran's Day Drive for Blankets and Shoes," taking it upon herself to go to every house in town, and every business on the square, to collect blankets and shoes for the veterans that served our country.

She always believed, "If the small-town people don't get out and about, they will think that there is no life outside the bubble of this one-horse town."

Cancer has a way of ruining plans. Just saying the word causes people to throw up their hands in disbelief, bewilderment, frustration, sorrow, and grief. I walked with Olivia and her family for the next nine months and witnessed the devastating effects of the "C-word." It tragically altered the course of Olivia's life, and it changed everyone else whose lives she touched as well.

At Olivia's funeral, I stood up with the family's pastor and the town's mayor right there in the middle of the Town Square. If you can imagine a Mayberry-like scene in the Andy Griffith TV show, then you are right on track.

She had me give her my word that I wouldn't be late, that I wouldn't wear a suit but rather, jeans and a western shirt (mostly because she knew that I don't like country music much and wanted to show me who's boss), and that I would give a message about how suffering loosens our grip on control. It was my job to comfort the town. She had put that in writing, given it to her parents, and instructed them to keep tabs on me.

I often didn't know how to effectively minister to Olivia, her parents, and her husband. As a young and green chaplain, my wet-behind-the-ears ministry was showing up. As a pastor, I had read books on how to minister to parents who feel forced to give up their children for adoption, parents who grieve the loss of their children due to drug overdose, addiction, and to pornography. I had researched parents in search of answers when their children were sentenced to incarceration. I had interviewed families who lost their children in a wayward notion drifting from the foundations of their faith and falling into the temptation of an illicit lifestyle.

Even though I had gained much wisdom over the years from studying and experience, I was struggling with coming to grips with what Olivia had said to me when she pulled me close: "No parent should have to bury their children." My own parenting skills were being challenged. I had even asked at one point along the journey if I could be reassigned to another patient, but my supervisor pleaded with me to stay on. I reluctantly agreed.

Many times, when people would encounter Olivia's parents following her loss, they wouldn't know what to do. Some would say things like, "Maybe God wanted her more than you," "You can always adopt," or perhaps the worst of all, "Would you like to have my child? I'm sick of their moodiness, complaining, or sarcasm." In the midst of not knowing what to say, we can say very harmful things.

Her dad pulled me aside while visiting him at their house a month after Olivia's funeral and expressed some of the great trials he was having— more in how people were treating them as a family than the actual death of Olivia.

He asked me what to do. He wanted to have a town hall meeting to discuss grief and let them know of their damaging words and actions. He wanted me to facilitate a TV program about the effects of a town that shuts down after a loss. I just listened and prayed for insight.

I replied, "Maybe the town is in grief and they don't know how to process their feelings. Maybe they need a way to begin. Maybe you and I can show them the way." I knew that he was interested because he began to tear up and said, "They miss my baby, too."

I spent the next two visits talking to Olivia's husband, his parents, Olivia's parents, her best friends, and I began to assimilate a memorial service for the town. Her dad insisted on offering the loss of other people to be included, so we added a time of remembrance for all those who were grieving the loss of their loved ones.

Children brought pictures of their pets that had died. The local junior high and high school made cakes and cookies to honor their loved ones. The girls basketball team got together to donate a new basketball court for the city park and called it Olivia's Park. Local farmers and their families lined the street with cars and trucks, adorned with pink and red ribbons (her favorite colors) to pay homage and bring about a spirit of memory.

The service began with the elementary school choir singing the National Anthem and Olivia's favorite Taylor Swift song. As they did, tears started to stream down the director's face and she had to sit down so the kids could go on singing. Another teacher from a nearby town stood up to finish directing the song. There wasn't a dry eye in the entire high school gymnasium.

The funeral home gave out pamphlets on grief. The volunteer fire department offered each person a rock that they had collected from the riverbed nearby to symbolize Olivia and others who had made a difference in their lives. The school staff and faculty from elementary to high school lined up with a banner made in pink and red with the writing, "Love is the Answer."

The stage was set. As Olivia's mom and dad were walking up to the podium to pray, her dad stopped and said to me, "We are about to make history." He was right.

Right there in the middle of small-town America, we were breaking all the rules, removing all the stops, and bringing down barriers with love.

When his wife spoke, she trembled in her speech. When he spoke, words were spoken with a firm tone. He stood tall as a towering, gentle man who spoke with dignity and honesty.

After a few more songs, Olivia's husband came up and spoke with great hardship and profound hope in his voice.

"I was surprised today by Olivia's joy. In the mail came a picture of our wedding day from a friend who doesn't live in our town. The shot came from an angle where she was looking at me with the eyes of a princess gazing at her prince. The caption on the back was astounding, 'Send this to him, it's what I want him to know every time I look at him.'" He looked up to the crowd and said in a loud voice, "Today let these rocks be a picture of what you are going through."

As he returned to his seat, I rose from mine. It was now my turn to speak. I slowly came toward the podium, offering one last silent word of prayer for the Lord to guide my words.

I stood before the crowd and started to stutter. I slowed down my breathing, and read Revelation 7:12,15–17:

"Amen! Praise and glory and wisdom and thanks and honor and power and strength be to our God for ever and ever. Amen!

"...they are before the throne of God and serve Him day and night in his temple; and He who sits on the throne will shelter them with His presence. 'Never again will they hunger; never again will they thirst. The sun will not beat down on them,' nor any scorching heat. For the Lamb at the center of the throne will be their Shepherd; 'He will lead them to springs of living water.' 'And God will wipe away every tear from their eyes.'"

I made remarks about how this passage of Scripture is mostly talking about the end of time, a great tribulation, and seal of God. It also has a very close and personal message for us: that as we endure the great tribulation of grief in our losses in life, change, transitions, the God who loves us will wipe away every tear.

My message was about God's peace, timing and comfort. I shared about how death, loss and transitions are hard work for people of all ages. I shared about how to talk with children, teenagers, and adults who are grieving. As I looked out into the sea of faces I felt as if I were speaking to a multitude, like Moses.

Scriptures that might be helpful when comforting people who are facing cancer:

A person's days are determined; you have decreed the number of his months and have set limits he cannot exceed. Job 14:5

Jesus said to her, "I am the resurrection and the life. The one who believes in me will live, even though they die; and whoever lives by believing in me will never die. Do you believe this?" John 11:25–26

For to me, to live is Christ and to die is gain. Philippians 1:21

But God will redeem my life from the grave; He will surely take me to himself. Psalm 49:15

My flesh and heart may fail, but God is the strength of my heart and portion forever. Psalm 73:26

Prayer Starters:

Oh Lord, You are our breath and life. Thank you for life as limiting as it sometimes is. Comfort my friends today as they find themselves hurting and in need of Your touch. Wrap them close to you. Remind them of your faithfulness and Your love for them from the very beginning.

Heavenly Father, You are the one who wipes our tears away. You come to my rescue with loving kindness and mercy. Sustain us now as we see with our eyes the pain of cancer and physical torment. Give us grace as we wait for your goodness to appear and remove pain and sorrow and enter into Your Kingdom. Teach us new songs of worship and praise during this time of waiting. You raised up Jesus, raise us up, Oh Lord.

Recalling Olivia

A full year had not yet passed when I heard from Olivia's mother. She shared about how the year had gone and the blessings of her church, her family, and life in the small town. She quieted down and stated that she had been cleaning out a box of Olivia's things and came across a note I had written when Olivia was asleep at one of my visits. She read the note to me, we were quiet, and she said that "today is a good day."

I agreed and hung up the phone after we said goodbye. It occurred to me that even though cancer is such a mystery, like so many other diseases, suffering through challenges and hardships can be a powerful lesson in living. I am a better person because of Olivia and her precious family. Her town is a blessed one–experiencing a richness of God's love, more than they ever thought possible.

Endings are not always like this. Sometimes families don't heal. Sometimes hardships rock the foundation so hard that pain and suffering are the end result, for decades. But the truth remains; God does some of His best miracles when we humbly trust Him; relying on His strength to stay the course, depending on His Spirit to help us keep running in faith, and remaining connected to Him by reading our Bible earnestly and praying honestly.

If you are struggling today or know of someone who is devastated by the events of illness, death, or a transition, be encouraged. The key is not in trying harder on your own strength, but in trusting more in His. Stay the course that God has for you. He is working out His plans beyond what we can often understand. God is making a way!

What you said:

"Maybe God wanted your loved one more than you did."

What they heard:

"God loves him or her more and wants to see me suffer."

What you wanted them to hear:

"I don't understand some things that happen in this life. I don't understand why God doesn't bring healing to the whole situation. I am here for you and want to support you and offer comfort. Can I pray for you?"

"I have realized I will now be less afraid to die because you have done it first. Whatever is ahead will seem more hospitable to me because I will think of you as being there to welcome me in— one more act of hospitality of the sort you have offered me all your life." Susan Ford Wiltshire (from *Grieving the Death of a Friend* by Harold Ivan Smith)

Chapter 5
Losing a Parent

Mr. Koy's Story

I received a call one Saturday while I was on call as a hospice chaplain. It was from a new patient who had come on service earlier in the week. I had made my initial contact within the first few days and said that I would be back in the next week to catch up with them.

(This assessment includes an introduction to the spiritual services offered by hospice, a chance to discover what the spiritual needs of the patient might be, and a chance to offer initial support as a plan of care was being developed.)

Mr. Koy had a diagnosis of end-stage liver failure. He was a happy man but was declining rapidly. His wife had passed away a few years prior, and they had three children: an older daughter, a middle son, and a younger daughter.

The children were in their late fifties. They were a nice family as I interacted with them on that first visit.

Mr. Koy didn't say much, and from the looks of it, his silence was due to his discomfort, which we were trying to manage and help get his pain under control. We were also preparing to move him from his home of 60+ years to a long-term care nursing center.

By the time all the arrangements were made for the placement a few days later, he was becoming quieter. It was obvious he was aware of what was going on as he moved his eyes across the room. I sat back down beside his chair one last time. I put my hand on his shoulder while the others were in the other room and asked about his favorite memory in that chair. I could tell he was thinking and then very quietly he spoke, "My children...them." As he pointed towards the adjacent room. I smiled and honored his words with silence. I offered prayer for him prior to leaving and we all joined together in reciting the Lord's Prayer. As I walked out, people thanked me for coming.

When I received the next phone call it came from my supervisor who stated that the nursing home had just called to request me. That was the first sign that something wasn't quite right. The second sign (or sound) I heard was three voices shouting over one another in a room around the corner from the door at the nursing home.

As I walked to the Nursing Station I laughed and said, "I hope that is not for me!"

While I pointed to the commotion, they pointed to the room Mr. Koy was in. Yup, that was the room. I received a quick update from the charge nurse and proceeded to the room.

When I entered, there were the three children standing by their father, whose head was upright and he was watching what was going on. My presence didn't stop their arguing and hollering like I hoped it would. So I cleared my throat and said, "Hi everyone, can I offer some assistance?"

They stopped for a few seconds and went right back to their yelling match. The only real words I was able to decipher were, "Truck, it was promised to me...and the hutch!"

I tried to use a calm voice to bring reason to them. I used all my chaplain training techniques, but nothing worked. My parenting model kicked in then, so I stood in the doorway and yelled out, "Stop it! Stop it! Stop it!"

They looked at me in disbelief. I stood there, also in disbelief (thinking that I could easily lose my mind and possibly my job). I then looked over to Mr. Koy and on his face were tears. I told the children to leave. Yes, I asked them to leave…and return in one hour with something that their dad had given to them. I asked them to take their personal items and go home. And they did.

For the next several minutes it was just me and Mr. Koy. His hands were clammy. He had a fever, and the nurse was coming in to administer more medicine. Our Hospice Nurse had already been there.

I noticed that Mr. Koy was not able to speak anymore. His breath was labored and his color and the function of his body were changing. I looked at him and spoke out about my sense of what he was going through, watching his children fight over the treasures of home. I told him I would probably be dismissed for yelling out at the kids and asking them to leave. He squeezed my hand softly. I knew at that point we were connecting.

I prayed for him while holding his hand, reading him the words of Jesus in John chapter 14. I could tell his demeanor was changing to a more relaxed and comfortable position. The nurse came in and repositioned him in his bed with more pillows and an additional blanket. I stepped outside to pray, asking God for a divine appointment and for wisdom when the kids returned.

The kids arrived and I had specific instructions for them:

1. Sit down in the chairs provided in order of age.
2. No talking unless you are asked. No eye rolling. No sighing. No form of non-verbal communication at all when another sibling was talking.
3. Put the item that you brought under your chair and be quiet.

The next hour went fast as I listened to the children share their items. The youngest child went first: "I brought this." And Debbie held up her wedding dress up on her shoulders like girls do when they are trying it on for the first time. "Daddy said that Tommy (i.e., the man she was about to marry) would leave me crying. Daddy said that he would hurt me, ruin me, and leave me lonely. He was right. Tommy did all those things."

I asked her what impact the dress had on her now. She stumbled out the words of a lonely young woman, "He bought me my dress anyway. He broke his own rule of not buying something he didn't believe in. But he believed in me."

It was quiet in the room while Debbie looked at her father and said, "Dad, I gave you a lot of trouble growing up, but you kept believing in me and welcomed me home each time." I held her dress as she hugged her dad. It felt heavy, as if the weight of the emotions it held had been stitched into the material.

The middle child, the only son, shared next. Shawn stood up and pulled out the rod and reel his dad had bought him. The others laughed and almost said at the same time, "I knew you would bring that."

I asked him to share the significance of the prized possession. Shawn shared that he and his dad would go fishing all the time. Sometimes, if Mr. Koy knew he could get away with it, he would get Shawn out of school early just to spend time together in the boat on the river's edge, by the lake, or wherever they could. Shawn said, "There were a lot of times when I don't think we even used any bait—but it was our time. I told dad everything, or he had a way of getting it out of me while we fished. But all was well, because fishing and pop was what we were about."

I asked if I could hold the pole. He showed me the difference between what it was and what they use now. He said, "I plan to raise up my boy the same way dad raised me—fishing."

The girls smiled. He was right. He walked over to his dad, picked up his hand, and shook it like two men do. Shawn wiped a tear before turning around and facing the chairs to sit down. Mr. Koy was also teary.

The oldest child, Kathy, was the last one to share her item in this show-and-tell journey. She had no box or item in a bag. Kathy was a rough looking girl, the only one that really looked older...much older than she probably was. She had a rather "leathered" set of hands, was obviously not afraid of hard work, and never married. "At least not to a person," she stated. "I married my business."

She then reached into her back pocket to pull out her wallet. She held up her driver's license. "Daddy taught me to drive," she said in a matter-of-fact way. "He taught me how to drive on the back roads of this city. He took me driving after church; let me drive halfway to school and a whole lot more. In fact, dad taught me to drive the Buick, the Ford, and that piece of junk International! He taught me to drive cars and to drive my business. When I was going to buy my first trade-in truck, he went to Oklahoma to get it. When I bought my first new truck to haul grain, he wanted to drive it first, and then followed me for a half-day to make sure it was okay. Dad was there when I bought out the guy in the business to show me how to run a business of my own. Dad was there when I hired my first driver, and when I fired my first driver."

She put her license back in her wallet, looked over at her siblings, and stated, "All this fighting is not worth it. Let's just be a family." She took a few steps to her dad, hugged him, and sat down.

I thanked them for sharing the intimate details of their lives with me and with each other. I offered to pray for them after reading (re-reading) John 14:1–4:

"Do not let your hearts be troubled. You believe in God; believe also in me. My Father's house has many rooms; if that were not so, would I have told you that I am going there to prepare a place for you? And if I go and prepare a place for you, I will come back and take you to be with me that you also may be where I am. You know the way to the place where I am going."

I explained that Jesus was encouraging his disciples (those who were the closest to him and followed him) that he was going to leave them but preparations were being made to provide for them something great. "Like Jesus did for his disciples, your dad has provided for you." I encouraged them to reach into their souls and discover what treasure he is leaving behind for them; a character—not an object—a value, not a possession to hold onto. I could tell the lights were coming on.

I left to return home on that Saturday to hold my family a little closer. I received word later that evening that Mr. Koy had passed away with each of his children by his bedside, getting along, and sharing stories of their dad and mom in a very positive manner.

Groundbreaking

The death of a parent is a groundbreaking grief. Like no other, it forces us to come to terms with our own mortality. A part of us is gone.

Gary Small observed the death of a parent in this way, "You never really feel alone in the world until you stand on your parent's grave."

Children who have buried their parent or parents have told me that they feel like calling out their names during challenging times—longing to hear their voice of reason and help. Others have wished they knew how to handle their own children the way they were parented.

Still, the most overwhelming need of bereaved adult children, grieving over the loss of their parents, is presence. Your physical and emotional "being there" creates support and peace. Presence has more to do with just being there than making up a few statements and hoping they come out right.

This groundbreaking feeling is easily linked with fear, confusion, and runaway anger that rips through our hearts and minds. Sometimes the best thing to do is to simply offer yourself, physically being present and not saying much of anything.

As an example of presence, I remember sitting in a church service where the woman and her children who were sitting next to me were fairly quiet and somewhat standoffish. The more I observed their candor, their behavior, the more I sensed they were in deep pain. Each of them seemed to have coverts of emotion, and no one had helped them. Perhaps this loss was too far gone. Perhaps it was so recent and so fresh that they were barely functioning.

I slipped a small, handwritten note to the woman with these words: "It seems like you are hurting. If you are, and you would like to talk, please call me and my wife." I enclosed my number and handed it to her. She smiled her best smile and kept her stare downward.

About two weeks followed without hearing from her. At these points I always want to know if I was too pushy, too much "touchy feely" which made it more difficult. But then on the way home from work, I heard from her, a text that simply said, "Thanks for being there for us. We are doing much better now."

I responded with, "Who is this?" And she texted back, "The woman crying in church with her kids." We exchanged a few more texts and to-day she is nowhere to be found. I'm not even sure where she is or even if I have her number any-more.

The moral of this story is that we just simply show up to be the hands and feet of Jesus when suffering comes.

May I strongly encourage you to do more lis-tening than talking. May I implore you to be there—to actually show up—instead of simply saying "I meant to come by but got busy."

Scriptures that might be helpful when comfort-ing adult children during their mourning:

The Lord is close to the brokenhearted and saves those who are crushed in spirit. Psalm 34:18

My flesh and heart may fail, but God is the strength of my heart and my portion forever. Psalm 73:26

For just as the sufferings of Christ flow over into our lives, so also through Christ our comfort overflows. 2 Corinthians 1:5

Show me the way I should go, for to you I lift up my soul. Psalm 143:8

Prayer Starters:

Dear Lord, You are the sustainer of life and the breath within me. I call to you for my friend who lost her mom (or dad). Thank you for the memories that she has of her mom. Thank you for the heritage and values of their character. Lord come close to her right now and remind her of your love and mercy...

Heavenly Father, You have a strong value for the people in our life that have birthed us, raised us, and trained us to walk with you. Lord I ask that you would make a strong pathway for my friend who is grieving the loss of their family member...

Remembering Mr. Koy

At the funeral of Mr. Koy, I sat in the front row with the children, at their request, as they each shared their gift from their dad like they did in the nursing facility room that Saturday. Now I wonder if Shawn is teaching his sons how to fish, and I wonder how Debbie is doing in her new life as a single mom.

What you said:

"It could be worse. You could be dead like them"

What they heard:

"I should have died too"

What you wanted them to hear:

"I am so thankful for your survival in the crisis".

"It is by those who have suffered that the world has been advanced." Leo Tolstoy

Chapter 6
The Challenge of Crisis

We Are Marshall is a movie that tells the story of the 1970 plane crash that killed the entire football team and staff aboard the charter plane returning home from an away game. It's a devastating story about a team, a town, and a university that felt loss from every angle. The portrayal of the decision to continue the football program there revealed the great pain, struggle, and truth to their suffering.

My friend Gene tells the story of what the catastrophic, mile-wide Joplin Tornado of 2011 (which killed 158 people, injured over a thousand others, and caused $2.8 billion in damages) was like for him and his church in a couple sentences: "It was the most horrific event that has reached my doorstep. Everywhere I went I felt the disaster...the might of this pain in my city. The wind at night will always be remembered."

When my daughter and I were out on our routine date night we were blindsided by a driver who thought he could make it through the light before we arrived in the intersection. He was wrong. We were wronged.

I can still recall the accident. Samantha and I were listening to music and talking about her day, and what we were hungry for as we were headed to dinner at a favorite restaurant. When the driver pulled in front of us, my foot hit the brake pedal and my arm threw out sideways to harness her back in her seat beside me.

As the airbag imploded she began to scream. The sound of crashing metal, breaking glass, and screams will stay in my mind forever. Samantha's words later are also seared into my memory. "I will never forget the day we had that accident, Dad. If you had not reached out your arm to me, my whole face and neck would have been bruised. Even with my seat belt on, you saved me Dad!"

My response? "Neither will I forget!"

The events of 9/11 fill our minds and loosen the tears of agony, defeat, and treachery within our souls to blur our focus, purpose, and placement about life and our meaning on this earth. The effects of crisis are often not limited by proximity either. We have been forever changed. We will never forget. Every time tragedy occurs, our life changes. Every challenge can turn us to reflect on our life. We are never the same after these suffering scenarios.

Carol's Story

After growing up around the redwood trees of Northern California, Carol shared with me, "We saw tall trees, big enough trees that a house could fit in, and trees that you could drive a car through the base. Those trees were the bread-and-butter of the area. Tourists would come from all around the world to see the trees, and it was my job to guide them through. This was where I lived, grew up, and where my family was born and raised. This is where I want to be buried.

"Anytime dry weather lasts for longer than a month, people of this area start to get nervous. Special precautions are made to not allow sparks from cars, avoid accidental fires, and to ban smoking anywhere near the woods. Campouts get cancelled, outdoor cooking becomes unlawful, and the park is even closed to the public at times. The California governor at the time, Deukmejian, declared a state of emergency in over twenty-two counties. This occurred in August of 1987.

"But fire still came, and it was uncontrollable. Everyone in those twenty-two counties was at risk. We had to shut down tourism operations. My job was on the line. My house was in the track of the firestorm. My family was being asked to evacuate. I remember being told (like we were warned days before) that we would be forced to leave.

"We had fifteen minutes to get our necessities and head out of harm's way. No one ever wants to be told to leave their home before it burns to the ground, but that is exactly what was being said."

As I listened to her, Carol took my hand, got up. and led me to a wooden Hope Chest. "This is all I have left. All I have left that's physical, that my eyes can lay sight of, is what's inside this box," she said with a stern voice. Let that sink into your mind!

I followed her instructions and grew quiet, having a deep respect for the places she had been. I wanted to get more facts, more stories, and more insight of what happened, but grew quiet instead. I was to let this sink deep into my life and examine what's important enough for me to grab when all hell breaks loose.

It was later, much later that I learned more about her family and that fire—this time from her daughter Kay. Kay shared her insights as a young girl in that fire, having to move from the red-woods to the Bay Area.

She goes back to visit every year on the day of her homeless journey. "That fire taught me lessons I'll never forget—faith, character, and beliefs."

Tragedy and Pain
"In this world you will have trouble." John 16:33

Interestingly enough and perhaps in a defining way, challenges and crises bring a definition to just how real life is. In a crisis our sleep is awakened, our eyes become wide, our hearts race, our breathing becomes erratic. We become keenly aware of our need for God, that life and all its toil is too big for us to carry on our own.

In a nutshell, during a crisis, we call out to God more than when things are going well and we 'don't need Him.'

It's helpful for us to keep in mind that a crisis is different from other types of grief. Crisis events are unexpected when they strike, unleashing their fury without warning. They are uncontrollable. They take our breath away.

Disasters, crises, and traumatic events are sometimes the hardest kinds to grieve over. Unfounded toil, unexplainable circumstances, and unreasonable thinking make these scenarios even more challenging.

What do I do? Why did this happen? How do I live my life? Where does this take me now? How much of this will be forever? Question after questions remain unanswered. We have an impoverished mental capacity.

Grief counselors call this kind of loss traumatic grief—a wave coming from an unexpected and tragic loss that catapults those left behind into an intensified level of grief. This type of grief is a direct response to a horrific event that threatens the safety, security, values, and beliefs around which we structure and live our lives.

What Not to Say

What we say to people after a crisis occurs is critical, and we ought to pay close attention. I've taken several crisis management courses and intervention seminars, and have taught basic to advanced crisis response workshops. The two overall and overarching care factors are (1) your presence and (2) that you are available to serve and advocate for their well-being. Physical, emotional, spiritual, and practical support is what is important.

I recall providing care to a family that was being evicted, and helping them navigate through their emotions and feelings of being homeless. As I was talking with their youngest son, I overheard a friend of theirs come over and say, "Okay so you are getting kicked out...this is just a home...you can find another one."

I literally got up and walked to the friend and asked him to leave. I was furious. How can he be so insensitive? This is where this family has had their children, grew in their faith in Christ, the kids were baptized in the backyard, and you think this is just a house?! The loss of a home is worthy of grieving and should not be dismissed as trivial.

"It will be all right" is another thing people say that they hope will bring hope. The problem with this statement is that it implies a time limit, and everyone who is suffering wants it to be over now. Rather than saying this cliché, perhaps a more fitting thing to say during a crisis is, "This time seems like it is hard. How can I best support you? I am sorry this is happening. Can I sit with you so that you don't feel alone?"

We can say a lot, but maybe that's the problem. We say too much.

Don't be tempted to plug some words into a sentence structure because you think something should be said. Sometimes saying nothing is more important.

When You Speak

Have you ever been in a conversation and said the wrong thing? My wife can probably point out more times than a few in which I opened my mouth and—well, let's just say it was not all that helpful. I guess I have had to learn the hard way about what to say, when to say it, and how to say it.

In grief situations I have sensed the same. I'm fairly sure that even as I am writing this right now, on a cold, dreary day, someone is listening to a conversation, participating in a dialogue, and thinking to themselves, "I need to say something."

I hope this chapter gives you some phrases to use while you are at the grocery store and you see the friend whom you have heard has just lost their daughter in an illness. I hope these pages encourage you to talk to your co-worker who is experiencing a transition in their home. I hope these sample sentences can equip you to know what to say in advance to the neighbor who has just told you that his mom is dying of Alzheimer's.

The table that follows is a sample of what I have heard people say over the course of my life—some to me, some about me, some to others. The NOT section includes phrases we say that are not helpful, not encouraging, and in some cases are downright rude and insensitive. Be cautioned; the odds are that you have said these. I have. We have grown up with them. We have heard our parents say them and our mentors repeat them. And in most cases you have never heard a backlash from these phrases, but if you were to tear back the layer of dialogue and possibly get into the mind of the receiver, you may hear things like:

"If I hear I know how you feel one more time, am going to scream."

"If someone else tells me they are sorry for my loss, I might just punch them."

"Wait for it, here it comes, wham! 'I've been there before.' UGH!"

The next table includes my suggestions for what to say instead. If you take a careful look, you'll see that some are very similar. Still, a closer look will identify the difference. You are making a personal and specific contact statement.

I call these honest phrases to say to people who are grieving loss and transitions. They offer more of your time and indicate more helpful listening. These honest sentences change the patterns of your conversations and cause you and the griever to move to another level of conversation. These have a way of digging deeper into one's soul and grabbing hold of what's really going on.

As you read these, pray. Ask God to help you say helpful and encouraging words as people open their hearts and share with you.

Also pray that you have a listening agenda, and that you become someone God will use to bring healing and comfort.

Not This	Try This Instead
"I know how you feel."	"What is it like right now?"
"I am sorry for your loss."	"I am sorry this happened." "I am sorry for (be specific)"
"That same thing happened to me."	"What is the most challeng- Ing thing right now?"
"I've been there before."	"What is affecting you most right now?"
"I know what you mean."	"Can you share how you are feeling right now?"
"I'll be praying for you."	"Can I pray for you right now?" "When I pray today, how can I pray for you?"
"Now you can focus on yourself instead of being	"Can we spend time togeth- er soon to instead of being

75

Not This	**Try This Instead**
bogged down for others."	enjoy a coffee or a meal?"
"Suck it up."	"I can tell this is hard for you.
"I am here for you."	"You are not alone."
"Look at it this way: there is always someone else feeling worse than you are."	"What are some of the feelings that you have today?"
"You matter."	"You are important to me."
"Let me help you."	"Can I give you my cell phone number?"
	"Can I give you a hug?"
"Stop feeling sorry for yourself."	"How is this time hard for you?"
"Stop feeling down."	"How can I offer comfort?"
"Maybe it's time to move on."	"What are some fears you are facing right now?"
"Try not to think about it."	"What is going on today that I can be here for you in?"
"I have no idea what you are going through."	"Can you help me under stand some of your feelings so I can be a good friend?"
"Aren't you tired of dealing with this?"	"There is no timetable for grief."
"Wouldn't you like to get out of this funk?"	"How can I support you?"

76

Not This	Try This Instead
"Have you tried…? (home remedies, a special tea, essential oil, etc.)	"What is something I can help you with?" "How can I care for you?"
"You should trust God more."	"What attributes of God seem to be the most present now?"
"Are you trusting in Jesus?" "Where is your faith?"	"Can I pray for you now?
"The thing you need to do now is…"	"How can I be a good friend to you?" "Is there an area I can serve you in?"
"He/she is in a better place."	"Pain is so hard for us to understand."
"He/she brought this upon herself."	"No one orders this kind of incident in their life."
"There is a reason for everything."	"I guess we may not know everything about the circumstance."
"You can always have another child, or adopt again." "You are young. You'll find love again."	"Nothing can replace your loved one. I am so sorry this has happened. Can I pray for you?"
"It must have been his/her time to go."	"Their passing doesn't seem right. I am sorry for this tragedy."

Not This	Try This Instead
"Cheer up; your loved one wouldn't want you to be sad."	"I am praying for you as you grieve. It's okay to be sad and cry. Would you like to have coffee and talk?"
"Snap out of it! You need to be there for your kids."	"What can I do to help you with daily routines, kids, chores, etc., etc.?"
Change the subject: "How About those KC Royals…"	"This is hard. I'm not sure what to say. I care about you. How can I help you?"
"I'll bring a meal.	"I'll bring a pot of soup and bread with those favorite peanut butter cookies you like so much."
"I don't want to talk about it unless you do."	"Would you like to share your memories?" "Whenever you want, I would like to listen to your memories and go through your treasures so you don't feel alone. I want to be a good friend."
"Everything will be okay."	"Can I come by with coffee on Tuesday?"
"Be strong."	"You don't have to be tough."
"Let go and let God."	"How can I pray for you today?"

Psalm 128:2 says, **You will eat the fruit of your labor; blessings and prosperity will be yours.**

I have always understood our words to be part of the labor of life. As a speaker and a teacher, my labor is my words. But through life in general, we speak into people: life and death, blessing and cursing. Let's be the blessings in people's lives as we open our hearts, listen to the Holy Spirit, and advocate for what God wants to do.

The words you speak are like an arrow, guided by the archer to the core of your target. What goes into the mind by our words comes out in a life

Scriptures That Might Be Helpful During a Crisis:

Since You are my rock and my fortress, for the sake of Your name leads me and guide me. Psalm 31:3

I will instruct and teach you in the way that you should go. I will counsel you and watch over you. Psalm 32:8

When my spirit was overwhelmed within me, You knew my path (NASB). Psalm 142:3

The Sovereign Lord will wipe away the tears from your face. Isaiah 25:8

For You have delivered me from death and my feet from stumbling, that I may walk before God in the light of life. Psalm 56:13

My comfort in my suffering is this: Your promise preserves my life. Psalm 110:50

Prayer Starters:
"Oh Lord, You have protected my friend's life from this calamity. Give peace and direction to her as she looks over the loss and pain. Comfort her with Your words of instruction and guidance."

"Heavenly Father, You are the giver of life and sustainer of breath. Come close and breathe life into my friend, who feels lifeless and unfocused. Strengthen her mind and call her faith to be awake in this dreary situation."

Remembering the Crash
My daughter Samantha struggled for weeks after our car accident. She had dreams of the crash and she talked about it often. Her teacher made a comment to her mom and me at parent-teacher conferences, "From what Samantha told me, if

you didn't put your arm out to push Sam back in the seat, her face would have been bruised."

I smiled and replied that I used my instincts as a parent and then brought my shirt sleeve back and looked at my forearm—its bruising was in her place.

Samantha couldn't get back in the car after its extensive bodywork was repaired. There were too many memories that caused her to be scared. One day, I stopped suddenly in a parking lot for a child and her look of fright came over my heart. I replaced the car that week.

She was skeptical but it was a new beginning.

I still move my arm instinctively across the passenger side when I have to stop suddenly, even if no one is in the car with me.

What you said:

"Now you can live your life instead of being a caregiver"

What they heard;

"Caregiving isn't very important and is not a noble act"

What you wanted them to hear;

"You have reserved the past several months to take care of someone very close to you. How can I bring support to you, as you grieve the loss of that individual and make steps towards a new normal?"

"Pain that cannot forget
Falls drop by drop upon the heart
Until in our despair
There comes wisdom
Through the awful grace of God."
Aeschylus

Chapter 7
The Forgetting

Darrell had been the one taking care of his mom and dad. He was the only child. Darrell was strong about his life, his faith, his love, and his affection for his parents. The one thing Darrell wasn't strong in was accepting his mother's Alzheimer's disease.

The hardest part about his day was knowing that when he came over after work to check in on them he would be faced with his mother not knowing who he was. He played it off well, but deep inside his heart of hearts he struggled with how something so mysterious could affect his mother so powerfully—the one who knew him better than any other person.

He would try to negotiate his feelings of being in a wilderness by making statements about the commonality of our own forgetfulness, especially when others were around. But it seemed that everyone knew about his heart breaking over the realization that his mother was dying a very slow death of Alzheimer's disease and dementia.

Eventually, with the help of his dad, Darrell moved his mother into a nursing home when it became apparent that she was not safe any longer at home. She needed more care. Plus, Darrell's dad was becoming more and more tired. There was more worry in everyone's mind as they wrestled with her being at home. Beyond putting her shoes in the freezer and the plates for dinner in beds was her need for security and safety.

Sometimes she would step out the door and walk for hours without anyone knowing where she was. At one point the police found her walking along the road with just a nightgown on. Darrell was embarrassed, but the overwhelming feeling of "my mom needs help" came as a stronger cry than his own pride.

For almost fourteen months Darrell visited his mom in the nursing home. Toward the end of her life, Darrell made contact with a local hospice agency that made daily visits, and brought forth a level of care that the family needed to be sure that his mom was okay. Her disease process continued to worsen.

Darrell continued to grow strong in his faith during these times, but his agony over his mother not knowing who he was hurt like he could never imagine. He memorized Bible verses and let me pray with him as his chaplain.

His wife was a strong supporter. His dad, struggling in his own way, was a support to Darrell and his 25-year-old son too. I recall one visit I made with Darrell where we all knelt on our knees and prayed for God to bring his mom home to Heaven. Three months later, God answered that prayer. After a long battle with urinary tract infections and pneumonia, she passed away.

Darrell felt a release. The next morning when I came to visit him, he had a smile—one that he hadn't had for quite a while. I asked him what had affected him. I was intrigued as to his stance.

He handed me a note that his mom had written to him years ago—the kind that you keep in shoeboxes to store for years to come. He was rummaging through a few envelopes, looking for an important insurance document, and he found it in an envelope titled "Darrell." The note read:

Dear Darrell,

You know that I love you. Even though the times you are seeing with your eyes are not going so well, know for certain that the love of God is in your heart and that your mom is your biggest fan. I may not always be around, so remember that God will. You are a special boy and I love you.

Darrell didn't tell me the specifics about the letter, but he did have a peace and calmness about him that morning. I asked him how the impact of the letter was to him years later. He replied, "The same as it did years ago...tears then peace. Mom is right; I still have Christ to comfort me, but my mom just said that she loved me."

I received a lesson that day. A letter from your mom is good any day, no matter when it was penned.

The Mysteries of Illness

According to the Alzheimer's Association (Check out Alz.org), "Alzheimer's disease is a progressive brain disorder that gradually destroys a person's memory and ability to learn or to reason, to make judgments, to communicate and to carry out daily activities." There isn't a main cause, but many researchers believe that much of the damage to the brain is affected years before diagnosis, which makes it feel undetectable. Scientific evidence is proving more and more that nerve cells that process, store and retrieve vital information to exist in a normal setting begin to be torn down by plaque and tangles of nerves, creating confusion, loss of abstract identification, and difficulty in speech.

While memory seems to be the first noted loss in the disease progression, it may not necessarily be all that is lost. Sometimes the person has the ability to dress themselves but not appropriately. Sometimes, in telling stories about their childhood, they may interchange their mother for their wife, their stuffed animal for their baby, and lose the ability to speak correctly about their passions as they did in years past.

According to the Alzheimer's Association website, the Alzheimer's Association statistics give evidence that:

• Approximately 4.5 million Americans have some kind of AD. 10% of those over 65 years of age and 50% of those over the age of 85 have AD.

• More than 7 out of 10 live at home.

• Family and friends provide almost 75% of the care for a person with AD. The remainder of care is paid in out-of-pocket costs costing an average of $1300 per year.

• Half of all nursing home patients suffer from AD or a related disorder.

• AD is the third most expensive disease in the US after heart disease and cancer.

• 1 out of every 8 baby boomers is projected to experience AD personally as a diagnosis.

It's helpful to see the facts straight when we are looking at a man in our office who is caring for a loved one, who is suffering from this mysterious disease. How do we give space to grieve yet also be supportive and offer help? How do we provide a Christ-likeness to a person like Darrell?

1. Reduce your own nervousness about Alzheimer's by learning more about the disease. By doing your own investigation by going to the Alzheimer's Association and others like it, you will see first-hand what you might be staring at in years to come.

2. Offer to sit with your friend's loved one while they rest, visit with other family members, shop, etc. In hospice work this term is called respite. Carve out a block of time to provide this "in your place" care to your friend's loved one. During the time of your visit, read your favorite story or the newspaper. Draw pictures or show them their own pictures throughout the house.

3. Without condemnation, remind them of their past but refuse to use phrases like, "You should remember, you ought to remember, etc." These kinds of statements only create a feeling of shame and judgment with a critical spirit.

Offering Scripture to Those Who Are Caring for an Alzheimer's Disease or Memory-Related illness:

I will instruct you and teach you in the way that you should go; I will counsel you and watch over you. Psalm 32:8

Show me the way I should go, for to You I lift up my soul. Psalm 143:8

May our Lord Jesus Christ Himself and God our Father, who loved us and by His grace gave us encouragement and good hope, encourage your hearts and strengthen you in every good deed and word. 2 Thessalonians 2:16–17

In Your name I will hope, for Your name is good. Psalm 52:9

Prayer Starters:

Heavenly Father, You alone offer life and breath to all mankind. My trust is in You. As I sit here with my friend I ask for You to bring about a confidence in trusting You like never before. Bring a strong hope for guidance and encouragement...

Lord, You are the giver of hope when it seems like no hope can be found. I pray for my friend as he sees with his eyes what his heart cannot stand to see. Give him Your eyes and Your hands and feet. Give him Your words to speak as he cares for his loved one. Show him Your encouragement. May his source of strength come from You…

Lord of Heaven and my life, I dedicate my friend who is caring for his family member to You. He is weak and full of hopelessness. Fill him with what You see and show him a vision for what is ahead…

Lord Jesus, would You do a miracle in this situation as my friend is struggling to see straight? Provide a miracle or a small break-through so that she can be encouraged. She needs a fresh touch from You, oh Lord. Show her Your love in a new way today. She needs You…

Never Forgetting

Darrell was brave enough to talk to me about the things he was challenged with as he was watching his mother suffer. His risk taking, vulnerability, and willingness to be open about his own feelings led him to be honest about his relationship with God and how suffering was impacting him. Today, Darrell stops at the nursing home each month with some sort of a kind gesture, to say "Thanks for caring."

Darrell will never stop grieving the loss of his mother. He is discovering a new normal. Not the

same, but one that includes writing notes to people—like his son—who just opened up a letter he
wrote to him on the way to class. I received one
yesterday.

What you said:

"It's been a long time. You ought to be over this by now. Stop dwelling on the past and look to your future."

What they heard:

"I am hindering myself by grieving. Stop grieving and start living."

What you wanted them to hear:

"There is no timeline for grief. I am here for you as a friend who can listen and encourage."

"When your life does not match the smiling faces on the holiday cards, it can add an extra layer of hurt during what may be an already difficult time of year. Some wish their friends and family understood the pain and grief they felt looking at families that were whole and happy." Mary Tyler Mom (from FamilyLivesOn.org)

Chapter 8
Grief and the Holidays

Grieving the death of someone loved is always hard, but during the holiday season it can seem unbearable. What if you don't feel like keeping up with your usual tradition? How can you cope with your pain when everyone around you is so joyful? How will you face the empty chair at the holiday table?

Happy memories are diluted by the pain and suffering of experiencing the holidays without a loved one who has died or transitioned out of our lives.

The Marshall Family

The Marshall family will never be the same. They have been changed for forever. The oldest son, Timothy, passed away overseas while serving as a Marine staff sergeant. His death shook his family and their circle of friends, like an earthquake in the middle of the night. No Marshall will ever forget the day the Chaplain and Lieutenant came to their house on Christmas Eve to "notify next of kin" of the unthinkable event.

Most of the family had been doing last minute shopping, while others were sitting together in the living room, talking, laughing, and thinking about their days ahead.

"When everyone gets together it's loud, sometimes crazy, and always fun," Mr. Marshall told me. "We were not expecting anything but more people to join the party."

So when the knock on the door came and they saw the military vehicle in the driveway, their hearts began to race with excitement. Mrs. Marshall said she ran past the door to see if Timmy was in the car or around the corner. She recounted how things had happened in the past.

"He was always making surprise entrances, you know." But Timmy wasn't there, and by the look on the faces of the men in uniform it wasn't good news.

The officers read the notification letter, offered care as best they could, and prayed. The whole family rocked with tears. Weeping went on for days. The entire Christmas holiday season had been altered...for good.

Timmy was a boy who loved seeing his family get together. He loved family meals, picnics with everyone and would often throw a party because everyone needed to put smiles on their faces.

Timmy's sister, Katy, says that Tim was the "party machine." He could turn any humdrum event into a party just by his smile, his loud voice of "let's dance," and his really funny way of dancing that would turn the mood into a celebration.

Young Timothy was a hero to many members of the family, but he was also very certain about his adopted mission to rescue lives from peril of all kinds. "War has causalities," Timmy would say to his family and friends. "I may not come back in the same condition, so you have to remember the purpose in your lives. I am going to live mine, you live yours."

But nothing that anyone else could say would make this raw pain go away. The Marshall family and friends planned and attended Timothy's memorial service a few days after Christmas and before New Year's day. Many people offered their condolences and brought meals, sentimental gifts, and encouraging words to the house. Time was soon enveloped by other events, and most people who knew Timmy got on with their lives.

"That took place two years ago and I still wrestle with Christmas and all the other holidays," Mr. Marshall told me. "Why can't I get over this? How come this pain is still in the front of my mind?"

And any holiday was always Timmy's big event. He helped his dad put the decorations on the outside of the house. He made it his practice to go to every one of the neighbors to greet them when he came back from his first tour of duty, and wished them well for the Christmas holiday. Christmas was his favorite.

The Trouble with Holiday Pain

The loss of a loved one hurts more on special days like holidays, anniversaries, birthdays, or whenever the normal routines of our lives are even slightly changed. The grief that occurs at these times has much more depth and mystery.

Such feelings are normal and to be expected. Holidays and special days intensify grief because they focus our feelings on the loss and the inevitable transition. The absence of our loved ones will alter our feelings, traditions, and possibly the very way we go about our lives during such days. In a very real way our memories will awaken and cause us to have sorrow...often more sorrow in our hearts than we might feel we can handle.

To make matters worse, during the holidays everyone has decorations, lights, and special foods and drinks. Everywhere you turn you are reminded of these holidays...but now without your loved one. Television, radio, newspapers, websites, and stores are all expressing their "joy" in this season. Everyone seems to be in great anticipation for each of the holidays to arrive, while the griever cannot wait until they are over.

Children and teenagers will struggle with holidays and grief differently than adults. They will need patience, as grief is unthinkable to them.

They may appear to be afraid, or they might feel intense sadness or anger and express various forms of rage.

Be steadfast in such times. Be as responsive as possible to needs of comfort and security, and give room for children and teenagers them to process this unique hardship. Teenagers need the support from parents, but they also need to be around their friends to help them cope. Be careful that you don't expect children and teenagers to spend the entire day with you during such holidays.

My friend, Harold Ivan Smith, wrote this in his book called Grievers Ask: "Sometimes, through tears, the grieving must say as sad a goodbye to traditions as they have to the people with whom they have shared those traditions."

Be careful not to put your own ideas or traditions in their place, though. Be sensitive to their situations and what they feel like they can participate in. Give permission to people to skip Christmas decorating, baking, and gift giving if it's needed.

Note: Holiday grievers are experiencing something everyone else is usually NOT. Give them permission to ease off the traditions. Invite openness in your own heart to feel some of their suffering.

Scriptures That Might Comfort Griever's Hearts During the Holidays:

I have become like broken pottery. Psalm 31:12

Even though I walk through the shadow of death, I will fear no evil, for You are with me; Your rod and staff, they comfort me. Psalm 23:4

For You oh Lord, have delivered my soul from death, my eyes from tears, my feet from stumbling, that I may walk before the Lord in the land of the living. Psalm 116:8–9

You hear, oh Lord, the desire of the afflicted; You encourage them, and You listen to their cry. Psalm 10:17

Prayer Starters:

Dear Jesus, the day You were born into this world as a savior is shut out for my friend. Heal their brokenness and collect their tears as they suffer the loss of their loved one. Be close to them as they discover a new normal in their lives without their loved one…

Dear Jesus, You are the giver of comfort and peace. As we read in the Christmas story of the Magi bringing gifts to You, may You come close to my friend who is hurting and grieving the loss of their loved one. Nurture a miracle in their hearts that they may experience the gift of Your presence through this holiday…

Remembering Timmy

Mr. and Mrs. Marshall and their family have created a "fun-day scholarship" within their community group that they are members of. Whenever they hear of a family within the group that is experiencing sadness, they seek permission to come over and offer a coupon of sorts. On the coupon it reads, "When you feel like you can, call the number on this card and a party awaits. We provide everything—you just show up."

Mr. Marshall says that it is a big hit. "Just last week we heard from a family that we gave the card to a year ago, and they wanted it for their new neighbor who just moved in from out of town."

The wife and Mrs. Marshall talked the other day and said that, "No one has ever done that before…and we are 53 years old."

Grief never loosens its grip on us when we say goodbye to someone close to us. But we can experience peace through comfort from the people who love us.

What you said:
"I know how you feel."

What they heard:
"BLAH BLAH BLAH BLAH"

What you wanted them to hear:
"I have experienced loss before but not this loss, not your loss, and I do not know how you feel. Can I listen and offer my friendship?"

"The Grieving begins the moment you hear the news, The Moment you mutter your first, 'Oh no!' And there will be many 'Oh no!' moments."
Harold Ivan Smith

Chapter 9
When Grief Strikes at Work

Seth's Story

"There is something special about a job well done that makes you feel great," David said to his team after he was told that they had won the Productivity Award for the quarter. He believed in hard work, a good, strong set of ethics, and the collaboration of a diverse group to accomplish all the parts necessary.

David's team consisted of five very different people, all having the same goals—to get the job done with excellence, go home, be a spouse, cat caretaker, or motorcycle rider, and come back to work. It was that simple. "We live at home and go somewhere else to work," he said.

One of the five, Seth, lived at home with his wife of six years. He had been with the company for almost a year, and had really proven himself to be a valuable player on the team. David recalled, "His work experience on paper showed us what we needed, and he came through. He pointed out potholes in our strategies, carved through a stack of papers to be compliant with, worked through a very tough interpersonal relationship with an opposing team member, and brought home the bacon every time we had a potluck lunch work session. That's why his firing blindsided us."

Seth had been stealing information, the strategies and hard work of the team, for one of their main competitors for several months. "It dumbfounded us," David said. "It took us by surprise so much that our boss sent us home to grieve."

David later said, "We didn't know what to do except stop in our tracks and get a head count of our causalities. Things like this only happen in Lifetime Movies. There isn't even a Hallmark card to send to a group like us."

He was right. What Seth did wasn't fair, wasn't right, and went against everything in the group's minds. After all, this was their livelihood, their bonus checks, and their families that Seth was dealing with.

David recalled, "All trust went out the window, and we had to begin again. We met at my home when my wife and daughter were at her folks, and we talked openly about the results of what had happened—just like a team would debrief after a game. We started over by laying out our allegiances to the program and to each other. It was time to pay the piper or call it quits.

"The next day the Human Resources Department came to both our staff and private team meetings to help us debrief, and to answer questions. On the Monday that followed came another surprise, another one of our team members was leaving…but this time out of choice.

She gave this reason: "It seems fitting that I begin my life as a stay-at-home mother now. I don't think I can take the pressure of working hard, to be let down like we have been, and not be the kind of mother and wife I need to be. I talked it over with my husband and my last day is in three weeks."

"Ordinarily we would have rejoiced for her," David said. "But it felt like another blow to the gut. She wound up working that week and calling in sick the rest of the days. HR came in again and said, 'It was bound to happen.'"

"The next day, HR disbanded the team and we all work in separate departments now."

This kind of grief is non-fatal yet still mind-blowing in every sense. The impact of grief on the workplace is great. When someone experiences loss, or experiences a major transition, everyone around seems to be affected. And because we work together as a team, our co-workers may have fatigue, experience a lower level of productivity, have the "blues," or seem to experience impairment in making decisions. These are normal characteristics of mourning a loss or a transition.

Co-workers and/or work groups can struggle with what to say, how to respond to bring aid or comfort to those suffering. How you deal with grief affects the grieving process greatly.

What Kinds of Grief Occur at Work

Employee family crisis, Wage structure change, policies, procedures, form changes, an argument that turns violent at the lunch room, a misappropriation of funds, trust broken, team shifts, being laid off, hostile takeovers, being passed over, co-worker illness, suicide, company relocations, supervisor harassment, employee stalking, bullying, and assaults can all cause employee grief.

What to Expect?

• Depression, withdrawal, short temper, absent mindedness, or exhaustion are normal emotions.

• You may have strong feelings yourself, especially if the loss or transition is "close to home" and one that you can easily empathize with.

What to Do?

• Set limits and boundaries. Most of the time people need to give each other space, room to talk (or not talk). If a co-worker wants to talk, suggest a specific time when you'll be able to listen with full attention such as a break or after work.

• Listen, but fully understand that you are not in the position to fix the person's grief.

• Help out if you can; take a shift or a responsibility for the short term. Be specific in your offer and tell your supervisor.

• Talk with your supervisor if you sense that your grieving co-worker is getting worse, talks about suicide, or exhibits severe dysfunction. Covering up this behavior does not help.

• Most important, don't ignore someone who is grieving. Think about the kinds of things you might feel and need.

• Create a memory board or a book of pictures or quotes, establish an online tribute via social media, keep a card in your pocket, attach a work approved pin to your lapel, etc., to give yourself reminders that "grief is going on here."

• Hold a special workplace only "Legacy Service" to share how another person's loss affected their life. Concentrate a segment of time acknowledging their unique relationships with loss and transitions.

Returning to Work After a Loss
Go easy on yourself.

Expect to be distracted or less productive than before your loss.

Take time out to grieve.

Give yourself room in your day to take a break and refresh yourself. Let people know if you need privacy or a shoulder to lean on.

Consider how much you want others to know.

Some people share with others as a way to cope. For other people, silence and solitude helps more. Some like to share only with certain individuals and allow them to be a broadcaster. Some sense that it is more important to join a grief support group, or to share within the context of a professional or a minister. Everyone grieves a little differently. Don't let others impose "their way" on you.

Keep in mind that you are grieving, and there is no one certain way it is supposed to go. Go easy on yourself and on others.

Be understanding with your coworkers Some coworkers—especially those who have never experienced what you are going through—will feel awkward and unsure of how they should behave toward you. Others will want to tell you all they know. Remember, they are grieving too and "just trying to help." As much as you may want to club them in the jaw, keep in mind that they grieve because you are grieving.

Keep your supervisor informed.

Know that your first few days back to work will be tough. Talk ahead of time with your Human Resources Coordinator and/or management staff and ask them to give you a "lighter load" for the first day or so. This conversation will create a safe space for you to operate. Be honest with them throughout these days.

Grief at work is hard to handle. Easy does it!

Scriptures to Share With Those Who Are Grieving at Work:

But as for you, be strong and do not give up, for your work will be rewarded. 2 Chronicles 15:7

Therefore my dear brothers, stand firm. Let nothing move you. Always give yourselves fully to the work of the Lord, because you know that your labor in the Lord is not in vain. 1 Corinthians 15:58

Since You are my rock and my fortress, for the sake of Your name lead and guide me. Psalm 31:3

Do not fret—it only leads to evil. Psalm 37:8

Cast your cares on the Lord and He will sustain you; He will never let the righteous fall. Psalm 55:22

Prayer Starters:

Heavenly Father, my friend has worked hard in his job and this time seems less than hopeful. Come close to him and call his attention to be on You and not just his situation. Draw near to him as he needs Your strength...

Lord, You are the giver of opportunity. Unhinge the doors of Heaven for my friend to walk through regarding his job. I pray that he would be faithful to hearing You...

Remembering Seth

About a year later, as David was at lunch near his office, he saw Seth across the street with yet another company, looking like he was employed there. He told me that he wanted to go across the street, punch Seth in the throat, and tell his new teammates what he had done a year prior. "But I didn't. I controlled myself (as he laughed). I'm a better man than that."

David has a new job too, supervisor of his department. And every year he gets the team together at his house and throws a team party in honor of the ethics and values that he has learned since the incident with Seth. "And what's cool," David concluded, "is that HR pays for it!" (We both laughed.)

What you said:

"I thought you were a Christian and had a strong faith"

What they heard:

"I am a loser in the sight of God and other believers. I cannot stay strong during tough times"

What you wanted them to hear:

"It sounds like you are experiencing some tough stuff. Can I pray for you? Can I ask God to give you more strength for this struggle? God's healing looks different in each person.

"Lord, if it's You, tell me to come to You on the water." Matthew 14:28

Chapter 10
Letting Go

Joey's Story

I was done speaking at an event in Chicago and headed back to my hotel when it started to rain. And, since I wasn't prepared for inclement weather at that moment I decided to hail a cab for the five-block trek back.

I got into the yellow cab and told the driver where I was going. He said nothing and started to drive. To be honest, I wasn't really paying attention to anything other than wiping off my glasses from the rain and thinking about where I was going to eat dinner. It was my first chance to be by myself all day, so I was enjoying the moment to slow down and process my thoughts.

That's when things changed.

About two blocks from my hotel, the driver of my cab took a call. I could tell right away that it was a personal call. Two reasons why I know this. One, he said, "Oh my God, are you sure?" Two, he floored it to my hotel while going through a red light and almost hitting a couple.

Believe me, this guy was flying. I had been in cabs before, and they generally do drive a little on

111

the maniac side, but this guy was hauling. He barely gave me enough time to get out the door and then he said, as he looked at me in the mirror, "This one's on me, pal," and sped off into the crowd.

My immediate response was to call him rude, but the hotel valet service man let me know otherwise.

"That's Joey. His son has been in and out of treatment centers for the past three months. He's overdosed twice and tried to commit suicide once. I bet something is going down and he needed to get to him."

I repeated his name. "Joey?"

"Yep," he said.

"Does Joey work every day?"

"Do you know a cab driver in Chicago that doesn't work every day?"

"Hmm. You're right. Do you know his contact information?" I said.

"Yep, sure do. We all got it," referring to all the valet and concierge staff.

"Good deal. When I leave for the airport, I'll have him drive me."

As I walked to the elevator, down the hall to my room and then to my bed, I was quickened to pray for Joey—not because I was a speaker at a conference and certainly not because I was a chaplain.

I was called to pray because God spoke to me about Joey, his condition, his agony, and his feeling of being defeated. I was called to pray for someone I knew for maybe eight minutes, because I desire to live my life listening to God tell me about people like Joey.

I didn't know then what I knew later, but God was preparing me for a divine encounter with Joey on the way to the airport. I didn't know what was going to take place, but God was setting things up for me to listen, to ask questions about his life, and to pray with him.

Lessons Learned

God uses people like me to help people like Joey.

You might say to yourself, "How can God use him when he only rode in the dude's car for eight minutes?"

I don't know everything to the fullest extent, but I do know that God uses you and me to help alter the lives of others going through loss. And, sometimes we just have to let go of our own agenda and be at peace with God's plan to use us.

For example, imagine yourself on a plane and you are just thinking about sleeping or listening to your music, reading your book, or just "zoning out." But there is this one person next to you whom God seems to be nudging you toward, to listen and hear—really hear—his story. And by the grace of God, you sense a call from God to let go of your playlist and tune in to what God has in mind for that flight...only to find that he just needs someone to talk to. He's in a desperate situation and he just needs a listener, someone who would engage with him and invest time in him for his benefit. He doesn't even need any advice, counsel, or someone to fix him. He just needs someone to relate to.

How about another example?

Let's say that you and your neighbor have arranged to have the play date at the park with your kids. It's every Tuesday after naps at 1:30. You always carpool together. You always bring snacks to share. She always brings a nice little piece of chocolate. You always give her your unused coupons. It's so routine and so "usual."

But today is Tuesday and her daughter is sick, and she calls to ask if you would still want to get together. You say yes, thinking that it's the regular thing, just a different location. You arrive to find her sitting in her chair, crying, feeling letdown because she feels like a horrible mother. You quickly discover that God has sent you to her to bring her comfort.

You are unexpectedly faced with a choice, to continue in a selfish or "business as usual" frame of mind or to let go of your own pre-conceived ideas and hold on to what God might be asking you to do. You are able to see this interruption as a blessing to this mom who needs someone to listen, cut out coupons, eat chocolate, and let the kids watch another rerun of Disney TV.

Can you imagine if the guy on board the flight didn't turn off his MP3 player and just sacked out with his free peanuts and coke? Can you see the difference it makes for another human being to offer their own life to another over coupons and chocolate?

These may or may not be life and death situations, but we don't know that, do we? The situations may not look like very big issues to some, but when God calls you to let go of your own agenda for a while, it often becomes a miracle of sorts in the lives of others...and in yours.

Turn the tables for a moment. What if it were you on that plane? What if you were asking God for a miracle of sorts, and to send you someone who could listen and really engage in a conversation? What if you were the mom who needed comfort and another woman's compassion?

Sometimes we have to let go to take hold of what God is inviting us to do.

Peter's Unbelief

Have you considered the passage of Scripture where Jesus walks on the water versus Peter's wavering disbelief, in Matthew 14:22–36? I wonder if we are all a little, or a lot, like Peter, somewhat in doubt? I wonder if we just need to have a Jesus on the water moment of our own to see that Jesus calls us to Himself to see things differently. Can you imagine if Peter didn't have that question? What if Peter wasn't even on the boat?

I really learn a lot from unbelief.

Peter had doubts. I have doubts. Peter had a hard time learning to trust in Jesus' words. I have had many times of distrust in the words of my Lord and Savior. Peter worried about what people thought of him. I sometimes let others dictate to me what's important.

Maybe this passage has more implications for us than first perceived. Maybe this whole new look at your life—letting go of your own agenda—is a good idea after all.

Now fast forward to the end of Peter's life. Peter led the church through a huge multiplication movement that literally changed its course. He became a rock star for the Lord in more ways than one.

Allowing God to use your minutes in the day, to be a blessing to another human being, can change the course of their story. Letting go of your own plans and schemes, to put Christ first, could make or break someone else's day...besides your own.

Joey's Story, Continued

When I woke up that next morning, I had Joey the cab driver on my mind. I still had to pack my bags, grab my muffin, and mocha from the coffee stand, and check out. But before I did any of that, I called down to my valet buddy. "Can you track down Joey for me? I want to personally request him to take me to the airport." He said he would try.

I received a confirmation call only to let me know that Joey was unavailable at the time of my request but could do it in 20 minutes.

"Done deal," I said. "I'll be down in 15." I threw all my clothes in my suitcase, tossed my laptop in my briefcase, and headed down.

Joey was embarrassed to see me standing on the curb, realizing it was me whom he had managed to practically throw out the night before. I smiled at him and told him that no one was going to take me to the airport better than he was. I gave my valet buddy a wink and got into Joey's cab.

Joey didn't last one single block before he turned around and quickly began apologizing for his driving and behavior yesterday on the way to my hotel. I sat back and prayed, "Lord I have a short drive to the airport. Do Your will. Here I am."

The next thing I remember is that we were having a full-on conversation about life's ups and downs. While driving like a bat out of hell, he was letting me in on some of the pain in his life. I listened. I secretly prayed. I listened more, asked a few questions, made a few comments.

Then I asked him, "Joey, who are we really talking about today?

He said, "Me. I am talking about me and my son."

And just as I was about to ask him to pull over, he blurted out, "But you don't have time to listen to my crap." I looked at my phone to check the time, smiled, and said, "My flight doesn't leave for three hours."

He said, "I know a place where we can talk and get some coffee."

"Lets do it," I replied.

It was the worst hot chocolate I ever had, but I sensed that I wasn't there for the drink. I was there for Joey. And for the next forty-five minutes, Joey shared about his teenage son, who had been in and out of treatment centers, rehabs…and last night, another overdose. This one scared him and his son so much. Joey even thought his son had died.

I listened with intensity as Joey tried to hold back his tears, how he was a single dad trying to prove to his ex-wife that he was capable of holding down a job and keeping his son. I listened to his story about how he was out of money, out of time, and out of luck. As I sipped the now cold hot chocolate, now even more horrid tasting, I asked him a question.

I quietly asked him how he is able to get through his days with the trouble he sees. His reply was priceless: "I have no hope anymore."

I saw the phone flash with a message that I had received. That also lit up the phone to let me quickly see the time. I had a little less than an hour to get through security and to my gate. I asked him if I could pray with him. He said yes.

I prayed a simple prayer asking God to show my friend Joey the way to hope. I asked Him to save his son. I asked God to show favor on the entire situation. I ended the prayer and he made the sign of the cross, giving an indication that he might be of the Catholic faith. He smiled and I smiled too.

On the short two-mile drive to the concourse, he thanked me for listening and asked me my name. I gave him my card and told him to contact me when he knew more about his son and how he was doing. He agreed, and let me know that he was on his way there now to talk to the doctor and staff about treatment. I smiled again.

Joey asked me to wait by the cab at the curbside of my airline's facility. I didn't realize what was going on until he and the curbside assistant came to me, took my bag, and gave me my boarding pass with an "A LIST" voucher. I looked up to them, and Joey smiled. "This is going to get you where you need to go, sir," he said. I smiled.

The curbside assistant took my bag to the conveyor belt and Joey put out his hand to shake mine. I put down my briefcase, shook his hand, and said, "You are a good man, a good father." I brought him close so as to whisper in his ear, "And your son will be proud to have you as a dad."

He looked with disbelief but with a glimmer of hope. I gave him the look that dads give one another when they are doing dad stuff. I walked away quickly toward my gate, and turned around just like a final scene of a movie, to saw him drive away. I breezed through security like I was a hot-shot.

I felt like a million bucks for those next few days, not for the fast pass through security and a good seat on the plane, but because God had changed a man's life. God used me to help someone else. God used me to share the hope of Jesus. It all started with me getting in a cab with a willingness to let go.

At the writing of this book, Joey is no longer driving for the cab company. He works on a construction crew outside of downtown Chicago and his son is recovering from several years of drug and alcohol use in a treatment center. Joey talks with his ex-wife with the hopes of reuniting. He attends a weekly support group of parents who have children who abuse drugs. "I have hope when I come to this place," he says.

Epilogue

These stories and others have changed my life in profound ways.

One of the implications of hardships is that they often make a round of changes in the care-givers, too. When life happens to others it also happens to us.

Sometimes these challenges have a way of shaping our core beliefs and values, while others simply cause us to reflect and say things different-ly, respond to our situations with more thought and perspective, or at the very least, make us re-member in a new way. It's not all void.

I hope you sense that through the lives of the-se people, you too can be changed. My hope is that as you have completed this resource you will have had an encounter with God—one that would offer change to you. That you would have more courage to serve the people that God would pre-sent in front of you...to have more boldness to care.

Chapter four of the book of Acts gives a pow-erful scene of agony in the middle of what looks like a defeat. Peter and John had just been re-leased from prison. It was a courtroom-like setting filled with rules and regulations. The men they stood before were looking to make an example out of these two servants of the Lord.

Peter was courageous in his speech, proclaiming that salvation is only found in Jesus Christ, and that no other name would save and give peace. And even after not being able to keep them quiet, the other men commanded Peter and John once again to shut down their operation.

"For we cannot help speaking about we have seen and heard!" said Peter and John, in Acts 4:20. Even more threats and they still could not contain their fervor. God had shown up in miraculous ways.

When Peter and John were released from the leaders they returned to the other followers of Christ. They informed them of what had happened and met together for a prayer meeting.

Take note of what they didn't say. They did not ask God to take them out of the game. They didn't ask God to strike down all those that were against Jesus. They didn't proclaim a hate march and plan for vengeance. But notice also that they didn't ignore what was going on.

Peter and John, and the other followers of Christ, asked God for more boldness. Acts 4: 29–30 says, **"Now, Lord, consider their threats and enable your servants to speak your word with great boldness. Stretch out your hand to heal and perform miraculous signs and wonders through the name of your holy servant Jesus."**

From the first time I sensed God speaking to me about pastoral care, offering comfort to those who were struggling or simply just wanting to be a "light" in the middle of other people's darkness, I have been touched by these words of "more boldness." My prayer has been, "Lord, open my heart so that I would receive Your strength and courage."

At a Loss was written for that purpose, to give hope to this decaying and heartbreaking world. I pray that it can be a great tool that God would use in the Body of Christ, to heal abandonment, other challenges of life, and offer comfort and refuge to those who are in suffering scenarios.

I commend you for wanting to read a book like this—to equip you and your friendship circles. As we conclude, may I pray over you one more time? I'd like to ask God to seal these words in your heart:

Heavenly Father, thank you for each one of my new friends who have read this book. Thank you for Your touch on their lives. Thank you for the way that you have carried them through their struggles, defeats, trials and hardships. Thank You that You have been their refuge, portion, and comfort.

Lord, as they come to the end of this reading journey, I pray that they would be strong and courageous, seeking You to be their help and comfort so that when their loved ones, friends, and acquaintances have hurts and are at a loss for words, you would fill their hearts and move them toward being a true empathetic friend, the way that you have called us too.

Fill them with Your Holy Spirit as they prepare for hospital visits, grocery store stops, park and neighborhood conversations, and long conversations over coffee. Give them more boldness as they reach out in love, the way You call us to, to be the hands and feet of Christ.

In Jesus' name, Amen.

Appendices

These appendices are a resource of collected wisdom from years of ministry. I encourage you to make use of them, and to refer back to them often as you comfort others through the journey of grief.

(A) How to Make a Hospital Visit

I can't tell you how many hospital visits I've made in my life as a chaplain, pastor, or simply as a Christian. It's probably in the thousands.

I have seen many hospital rooms, spent hours in stale, stuffy waiting rooms, strolled through a ton of overpriced gift shops, ate a lot of over-cooked meals in cafeterias, dropped countless quarters into vending machines, and walked the halls with many families. And, if you press me, I bet I can find just about anything in a hospital building by just showing up at the front door.

Knowing how to make a visit to the hospital, clinic, hospice, or treatment center is vitally important in a comfort giving relationship. One of these days you will be asked to visit on your own, or to come alongside someone else going...and waiting in the car just doesn't seem to be such a great idea. Or worse, you will be in the hospital room and want someone to visit you, but they are all in the parking lot wondering how to make it short and sweet, kind of like a drive–in visit.

"I'll tell you what I want, you receive it, and I'll be on my way."

In these hospital rooms, you will smell things that won't be pleasing. You might hear some things that make you never want to return. Let's face it...hospitals, treatment centers, and clinics can be miserable places to be. But they are a great place to offer care, give support, and be a blessing.

For the most part, people who are in these rooms probably do not want to be there. They are constantly poked, asked the same questions, and cannot do as they please. They are tired due to the lack of sleep, weary from medicine interactions, and sometimes not as lucid as they normally are. They need you to come by to create an environment of encouragement, support, and love. They want interaction from their friends and loved ones.

Feel free to use this outline to give aid to your visit to the hospital. Allow these things to guide your time and set you up to succeed. May the Lord use you in a mighty way as you enter the doors of that room to visit your loved one, to be empathetic and fully present, to be there for just the right amount of time, and for the patient and their family to be encouraged.

In advance

1. Prepare for your time, in prayer. On your own you can be a great voice of reason, make them laugh, and create a moment for them to appreciate wonderful attributes of character. However, you run the risk of just being noise if you don't join in with what God wants for you to do. Ask the Lord what His agenda is for your visit, and plan accordingly.

2. As you sense the Lord leading, prepare a small passage of Scripture that you will be ready to share if appropriate. Have it ready on your Bible app on your phone. Plan for poor Internet service, and have a backup plan with a small little Bible you could put in your car for these reasons. Be sure the Scripture is something that is encouraging and uplifting. Use the Scriptures in the following pages of this appendix and given throughout this book.

3. Call the family to be sure the time you have chosen to visit works well with them, the nursing staff, visiting hours, and overall general flow of the day. Keep in mind that the first few hours of arrival are not good times to visit your friends in the hospital. Give the nurses and techs the time they need to get acquainted with their new patient, set them up with the equipment they need and get them adjusted to the medicine. Also, it is a good idea to be aware of the nurses and other staff that are coming off their shifts and coming on. This time is called "giving report" and usually takes two hours. Avoid coming during this time, as it only creates chaos for everyone. Also note that if you find yourself only able to come during these times, ask the family to meet you in the lobby or cafeteria to stay out of the way of the staff. They need to do their work. Even the paid chaplains and social workers abide by this rule.

4. If you want to bring flowers or balloons to the room, be sure to ask permission from the nurse first. I can't tell you how many times I have seen family and friends bring these wonderful articles of love, yet have to be thrown out because they create negative interactions to the medicine the patients are taking, fill up too much space in the room, etc. For instance, some of the metallic balloons are forbidden in the hospitals due to the materials from which they are made. Find out ahead of time what is allowed.

5. If you are sick or have an infection of any kind, your phone call is the best kind of visit. I urge you to not visit if you are sick. Your friend doesn't need the increased chance of becoming contaminated by your sickness, as they are trying to heal from their own illness or procedure.

At the visit

1. Check in with the nurses or aids on staff prior to entering the room. This will keep you from walking in during a bath, while the patient is using the restroom, or just an awkward moment. Believe me, they don't want you to see some of the things the nurses and techs are doing. It's better just to wait out in the hall.

2. Be aware of isolation, infection control, and general hand washing regiments as you enter. Checking in with the nurse will help you in this as well. Washing your hands and/or using germicide types of sanitation is always a good practice.

3. Knock prior to entry. Keep in mind, this is their "home away from home" right now. You wouldn't just barge into their home in a regular setting, right? Avoid the "surprise" visit. Knock and let them welcome you or ask you to visit another time. Sometimes other things go, on and all visits are postponed due to medical reasons. Abide by the rules and be flexible.

4. A note about length of stay. Plan to visit no less than ten or fifteen minutes, but don't stay longer than forty-five minutes. Many times, these patients are tired and may only be able to talk or stay alert for short moments at a time. Be supportive and empathetic to these types of situations. If they want you to stay longer, be sure to use your best judgment.

5. When you get there, ask how things are going, what challenges they have, and what are the doctors and nurses saying about recovery, diagnosis, etc. Asking questions like these will help break the ice in providing care and can positively improve your visit. Other things you can do include bringing a DVD to watch, a video game to play, a deck of cards, etc. Musical instruments are good to use, too, providing they're not too loud for the other patients/residents. Offer to read Scripture and to pray with everyone in the room as a group.

6. Offer to get something for the patient and family, including books, puzzles, coffee, water, snacks, etc.

7. If the patient you are visiting has a roommate and you sense that he or she would benefit from spiritual care, be open to that.

Conclusion (as you leave)
1. Thank the patient and family for allowing you to visit. Ask if it's okay to return another day.

2. Thank the nursing and tech staff on duty.

3. Consider making contact with your church's care pastor or lead pastor (if appropriate) to report your visit. This type of communication keeps your leaders in the loop for care and prayer.

(B) Scriptures on…

The Bible is overflowing with wisdom and knowledge! Whatever the problem, concern, or question may be, God has provided victorious guidance and instruction in the inspired writings contained in His Word.

These verses should be used in a relational mindset, and not as a foolish "Bible thumping" method for pushing someone to repent. Allow the Holy Spirit to guide and empower you to use the Scriptures with discernment, love, and a prophetic nature.

Scriptures on "Grief"

The LORD is close to the brokenhearted and saves those who are crushed in spirit. Psalm 34:18

The Sovereign LORD will wipe away the tears from all faces. Isaiah 25:8

He heals the brokenhearted and binds up their wounds. Psalm 147:3

Surely he took up our infirmities and carried our sorrows. Isaiah 53:4

My soul is weary with sorrow; strengthen me according to your word. Psalm 119:28

Death is the destiny of every man; the living should take this to heart. Ecclesiastes 7:2

Brothers, we do not want you to be ignorant about those who fall asleep, or to grieve like the rest of men, who have no hope. I Thessalonians 4:13

We believe that Jesus died and rose again and so we believe that God will bring with Jesus those who have fallen asleep in him. 1 Thessalonians 4:14

For this very reason, Christ died and returned to life so that he might be the Lord of both the dead and the living. Romans 14:9

Scriptures on "Death and Dying"

For he must reign until he has put all his enemies under his feet. The last enemy to be destroyed is death. 1 Corinthians 15:25–26

I declare to you, brothers, that flesh and blood cannot inherit the kingdom of God, nor does the perishable inherit the imperishable. 1 Corinthians 15:50

Listen, I tell you a mystery: We will not all sleep, but we will all be changed--in a flash, in the twinkling of an eye, at the last trumpet. 1 Corinthians 15:51–52

Where, O death, is your sting? Where O death, is your victory? 1 Corinthians 15:55

No man has power over the wind to contain it; so no one has power over the day of his death. Ecclesiastes 8:8

I will ransom them from the power of the grave; I will redeem them from death. Where, O death, are your plagues? Where, O grave is your destruction? Hosea 13:14

Those who walk uprightly enter into peace; they find rest as they lie in death. Isaiah 57:2

Man's days are determined; you have de-creed the number of his months and have set limits he cannot exceed. Job 14:5

For God so loved the world that he gave his one and only Son, that whoever believes in him shall not perish but have eternal life. John 3:16

I tell you the truth, a time is coming and has now come when the dead will hear the voice of the Son of God and those who hear will live. John 5:25

I tell you the truth, if anyone keeps my word, he will never see death. John 8:51

I am the resurrection and the life. He who believes in me will live, even though he dies; and whoever lives and believes in me will never die. John 11:25–26

And if I go and prepare a place for you, I will come back and take you to be with me that you also may be where I am. John 14:3

He is not the God of the dead, but of the liv-ing for to him all are alive. Luke 20:38

For to me, to live is Christ and to die is gain. Philippians 1:21

Even though I walk through the valley of the shadow of death, I fear no evil, for you are with me; your rod and your staff, they comfort me. Psalm 23:4

But the eyes of the LORD are on those who fear him, on those whose hope is in his unfailing love, to deliver them from death and keep them alive in famine. Psalm 33:18–19

But God will redeem my life from the grave; he will surely take me to himself. Psalm 49:15

For you have delivered me from death and my feet from stumbling, that I may walk before God in the light of my life. Psalm 56:13

Our God is a god who saves; from the Sovereign LORD comes escape from death. Psalm 68:20

My flesh and my heart may fail, but God is the strength of my heart and my portion forever. Psalm 73:26

For I am convinced that neither death nor life, neither angels nor demons, neither the present nor the future, nor any powers, neither height nor depth, nor anything else in all creation, will be able to separate us from the love of

God that is in Christ Jesus our Lord. Romans 8:38–39

If we live, we live to the Lord; and if we die, we die to the Lord. So, whether we live or die, we belong to the Lord. Romans 14:8

Scriptures on "Suffering"

I have suffered much. Psalm 119:107

I have become like broken pottery. Psalm 31:12
Look upon my affliction and my distress and take away all my sins. Psalm 25:18

I have suffered much; preserve my life, LORD, according to your word. Psalm 119:107

Look upon my suffering and deliver me, for I have not forgotten your law. Psalm 119:153

You hear, O LORD, the desire of the afflicted; you encourage them, and you listen to their cry. Psalm 10:17

In my anguish I cried to the LORD, and he answered by setting me free. Psalm 118:5

I will be glad and rejoice in your love, for you saw my affliction and knew the anguish of my soul. Psalm 31:7

For he has not despised or disdained the suffering of the afflicted one; he has not hidden his face from him but has listened to his cry for help. Psalm 22:24

My comfort in my suffering is this: Your promise preserves my life. Psalm 119:50

For just as the sufferings of Christ flow over into our lives, so also through Christ our comfort overflows. 2 Corinthians 1:5

He was despised and rejected by men, a man of sorrows, and familiar with suffering. Isaiah 53:3

Therefore, since Christ suffered in his body, arm yourselves also with the same attitude, because he who has suffered in his body is done with sin. As a result, he does not live the rest of his earthly life for evil human desires, but rather for the will of God. 1 Peter 4:1–2

Make us glad for as many days as you have afflicted us, for as many years as we have seen trouble. Psalm 90:15

Surely it was for my benefit that I suffered such anguish. Isaiah 38:17

It was good for me to be afflicted so that I might learn your decrees. Psalm 119:71

I have tested you in the furnace of affliction. Isaiah 48:10

We also rejoice in our sufferings, because we know that suffering produces perseverance; perseverance, character; and character, hope. Romans 5:3–4

I consider that our present sufferings are not worth comparing with the glory that will be joy revealed in us. Romans 8:18

And the God of all grace, who called you to his eternal glory in Christ, after you have suffered a little while, will himself restore you and make you strong, firm and steadfast. 1 Peter 5:10

Scriptures on "Sickness"

I am in pain and distress; may your salvation, O God, protect me. Psalm 69:29

Be merciful to me, LORD, for I am faint; O LORD, heal me, for my bones are in agony. Psalm 6:2

Heal me, O LORD, and I will be healed; save me and I will be saved, for you are the one I praise. Jeremiah 17:14

O LORD my God, I called to you for help and you healed me. Psalm 30:2

My soul will boast in the LORD; let the afflicted hear and rejoice. Psalm 34:2

For he will deliver the needy who cry out, the afflicted who have no one to help. Psalm 72:12

The LORD will sustain him on his sickbed and restore him from his bed of illness. Psalm 41:3

When the sun was setting, the people brought to Jesus all who had various kinds of sickness, and laying his hands on each one, he healed them. Luke 4:40

And the people all tried to touch him, because power was coming from him and healing them all. Luke 6:19

Jesus had compassion on them and touched their eyes. Immediately they received their sight and followed him. Matthew 20:34

The blind and the lame came to him at the temple, and he healed them. Matthew 21:14

Is any of you sick? He should call the elders of the church to pray over him and anoint him with oil in the name of the Lord. James 5:14

And the prayer offered in faith will make the sick person well; the Lord will raise him up. James 5:15

Scriptures on "Hardships"

Be joyful always; pray continually; give thanks in all circumstances, for this is God's will for you in Christ Jesus. 1 Thessalonians 5:16–18

Endure hardship with us like a good soldier of Christ Jesus. 2 Timothy 2:3

When times are good, be happy; but when times are bad, consider: God has made the one as well as the other. Ecclesiastes 7:14

Light is sweet, and it pleases the eyes to see the sun. However many years a man may live, let him enjoy them all. But let him remember the days of darkness, for they will be many. Ecclesiastes 11:7–8

Endure hardship as discipline; God is treating you as sons. For what son is not disciplined by his father? Hebrews 12:7

Blessed is the man who perseveres under trial, because when he has stood the test, he will receive the crown of life that God has promised to those who love him. James 1:12

I will continue to rejoice, for I know that through your prayers and the help given by the

Spirit of Jesus Christ, what has happened to me will turn out for my deliverance. Philippians 1:18–19

Praise be to the Lord, to God our Savior, who daily bears our burdens. Psalm 68:19

Scriptures on "Sorrow"

Godly sorrow brings repentance that leads to salvation and leaves no regret, but worldly sorrow brings death. 2 Corinthians 7:10

They will enter Zion with singing; everlasting joy will crown their heads. Gladness and joy will overtake them, and sorrow and sighing will flee away. Isaiah 35:10

Surely he took up our infirmities and carried our sorrows. Isaiah 53:4

Jesus wept. John 11:35

Blessed are you who weep now, for you will laugh. Luke 6:21

My soul is overwhelmed with sorrow to the point of death. Stay here and keep watch with me. Matthew 26:38

A happy heart makes the face cheerful, but heartache crushes the spirit. Proverbs 15:13

A cheerful heart is good medicine, but a crushed spirit dries up the bones. Proverbs 17:22

My soul is weary with sorrow; strengthen me according to your word. Psalm 119:28

Why are you downcast, O my soul? Why so disturbed within me? Put your hope in God, for I will yet praise Him, my Savior and my God. Psalms 43:5

Scriptures on "Guidance"

I will instruct you and teach you in the way you should go; I will counsel you and watch over you. Psalm 32:8

I know, O LORD, that a man's life is not his own; it is not for man to direct his steps. Jeremiah 10:23

Teach me your way, O LORD, and I will walk in your truth. Psalm 86:11

Show me the way I should go, for to you I lift up my soul. Psalm 143:8

Send forth your light and your truth, let them guide me; let them bring me to your holy mountain, to the place where you dwell. Psalm 43:3

Teach me your way, O LORD; lead me in a straight path because of my oppressors. Psalm 27:11

Direct my footsteps according to your word; let no sin rule over me. Psalm 119:133

Since you are my rock and my fortress, for the sake of your name lead and guide me. Psalm 31:3

Lead me, O LORD, in your righteousness because of my enemies— make straight your way before me. Psalm 5:8

Scriptures on "Having God's Image"

Then God said, "Let us make man in our image, in our likeness, and let them rule over the fish of the sea and the birds of the air, over the livestock, over all the earth, and over all the creatures that move along the ground." Genesis 1:26

So God created man in his own image, in the image of God he created him; male and female he created them. Genesis 1:27

O LORD, You are our Father. Isaiah 64:8

We are His offspring .Acts 17:28

The Spirit of God has made me; the breath of the Almighty gives me life. Job 33:4

Rich and poor have this in common: the LORD is the maker of them all. Proverbs 22:2

And just as we have born the likeness of the earthly man, so shall we bear the likeness of the man from heaven. 1 Corinthians 15:49

And we, who with unveiled faces all reflect the Lord's glory, are being transformed into his likeness with ever-increasing glory, which

comes from the Lord, who is the Spirit. 2 Corinthians 3:18

In this way, love is made complete among us so that we will have confidence on the Day of Judgment, because in this world we are like him. 1 John 4:17

For we are God's workmanship, created in Christ Jesus to do good works, which God prepared in advance for us to do. Ephesians 2:10

And we are in Him who is true - even in His Son Jesus Christ. 1 John 5:20

You made him ruler over the works of Your hands; You put everything under his feet. Psalm 8:6

The very hairs of your head are numbered. Luke 12:7

When I consider Your heavens, the work of Your fingers, the moon and the stars, which You have set in place, what is man that You are mindful of him, and the son of man that You care for him? Psalm 8:3–4

You made him a little lower than the heavenly beings and crowned him with glory and honor. Psalm 8:5

Scriptures on "Hopelessness"

Anyone who is among the living has hope. Ecclesiastes 9:4

Why are you downcast, O my soul? Why so disturbed within me? Put your hope in God, for I will yet praise Him, my Savior and my God. Psalms 43:5

Praise be to the God and Father of our Lord Jesus Christ! In his great mercy He has given us new birth into a living hope through the resurrection of Jesus Christ from the dead. 1 Peter 1:3

May our Lord Jesus Christ himself and God our Father, who loved us and by His grace gave us eternal encouragement and good hope, encourage your hearts and strengthen you in every good deed and word. 2 Thessalonians 2:16–17

Find rest, O my soul, in God alone; my hope comes from Him. Psalm 62:5

Sustain me according to Your promise, and I will live; do not let my hopes be dashed. Psalm 119:116

May Your unfailing love rest upon us, O LORD, even as we put our hope in You. Psalm 33:22

For You have been my hope, O Sovereign LORD, my confidence since my youth. Psalm 71:5

In Your name I will hope, for Your name is good. Psalm 52:9

No one whose hope is in You will ever be put to shame. Psalm 25:3

You are God my Savior, and my hope is in You all day long. Psalm 25:5

Why are you downcast, O my soul? Why so disturbed within me? Put your hope in God, for I will yet praise Him, my Savior and my God. Psalms 43:5 Psalm 65:5

Why are you downcast, O my soul? Why so disturbed within me? Put your hope in God, for I will yet praise Him, my Savior and my God. Psalms 43:5Psalm 37:9

But hope that is seen is no hope at all. Who hopes for what he already has? But if we hope for what we do not yet have, we wait for it patiently. Romans 8:24–25

I have put my hope in Your word. Psalm 119:74

For everything that was written in the past was written to teach us, so that through endurance and the encouragement of the Scriptures we might have hope. Romans 15:4

I pray also that the eyes of your heart may be enlightened in order that you may know the hope to which He has called you, the riches of His glorious inheritance in the saints, and His incomparably great power for us who believe. Ephesians 1:18–19

There is one body and one Spirit—just as you were called to one hope when you were called—one Lord, one faith, one baptism; one God and Father of all, who is over all and through all and in all. Ephesians 4:4–6

Therefore, since we have such a hope, we are very bold. 2 Corinthians 3:12

Always be prepared to give an answer to everyone who asks you to give the reason for the hope that you have. But do this with gentleness and respect, keeping a clear conscience, so that those who speak maliciously against your good behavior in Christ may be ashamed of their slander. 1 Peter 3:15–16

153

But as for me, I will always have hope; I will praise You more and more. Psalm 71:14

May the God of hope fill you with all joy and peace as you trust in Him, so that you may overflow with hope by the power of the Holy Spirit. Romans 15:13

Scriptures on "the Elderly"

Rise in the presence of the aged, show respect for the elderly and revere your God. I am the LORD. Leviticus 19:32

Is not wisdom found among the aged? Does not long life bring understanding? Job 12:12

Gray hair is a crown of splendor; it is attained by a righteous life. Proverbs 16:31

The glory of young men is their strength, gray hair the splendor of the old. Proverbs 20:29

Children's children are a crown to the aged. Proverbs 17:6

Teach the older men to be temperate, worthy of respect, self-controlled, and sound in faith, in love and in endurance. Then they can train the younger women to love their husbands and children, to be self-controlled and pure, to be busy at home, to be kind, and to be subject to their husbands, so that no one will malign the word of God. Titus 2:2–5

Do not cast me away when I am old; do not forsake me when my strength is gone. Psalm 71:9

Even when I am old and gray, do not forsake me, O God, till I declare your power to the next generation, your might to all who are to come. Psalm 71:18

Scriptures on "Encouraging Adolescents"

Don't let anyone look down on you because you are young, but set an example for the believers in speech, in life, in love, in faith and in purity. 1 Timothy 4:12

Be happy, young man, while you are young, and let your heart give you joy in the days of your youth. Follow the ways of your heart and whatever your eyes see, but know that for all these things, God will bring you to judgment. Ecclesiastes 11:9

Hold on to instruction, do not let it go; guard it well, for it is your life. Proverbs 4:13

My son, preserve sound judgment and discernment, do not let them out of your sight; they will be life for you, an ornament to grace your neck. Then you will go on your way in safety, and your foot will not stumble; when you lie down, you will not be afraid; when you lie down, your sleep will be sweet. Proverbs 3:21–24

My son, if your heart is wise, then my heart will be glad; my inmost being will rejoice when your lips speak what is right. Proverbs 23:15–16

My son, keep your father's commands and do not forsake your mother's teaching. Bind them upon your heart forever; fasten them around your neck. When you walk, they will guide you; when you sleep, they will watch over you; when you awake, they will speak to you. Proverbs 6:20–22

Listen to advice and accept instruction, and in the end you will be wise. Proverbs 19:20

Listen, my son, and be wise, and keep your heart on the right path. Proverbs 23:19

My son, give me your heart and let your eyes keep to my ways. Proverbs 23:26

Be wise, my son, and bring joy to my heart. Proverbs 27:11

He who walks with the wise grows wise, but a companion of fools suffers harm. Proverbs 13:20

Do not be misled: "Bad company corrupts good character." 1 Corinthians 15:33

My son, if sinners entice you, do not give in to them. Proverbs 1:10

Honor your father and mother...so that it may go well with you and that you may enjoy long life on the earth. Ephesians 6:2

Children, obey your parents in everything, for this pleases the Lord. Colossians 3:20

May your father and mother be glad; may she who gave you birth rejoice! Proverbs 23:25

Since my youth, O God, you have taught me, and to this day I declare your marvelous deeds. Psalm 71:17

How can a young man keep his way pure? By living according to your word. Psalm 119:9

Scriptures on "Anxiety, Fear, and Worry "

Cast all your anxiety on Him because He cares for you. 1 Peter 5:7

Do not be anxious about anything, but in everything, by prayer and petition, with thanksgiving, present your requests to God. And the peace of God, which transcends all understanding, will guard your hearts and your minds in Christ Jesus. Philippians 4:6-7

Do not fret—it leads only to evil. Psalm 37:8

Martha, Martha, the Lord answered, you are worried and upset about many things, but only one thing is needed. Mary has chosen what is better, and it will not be taken away from her. Luke 10:41–42

For God did not give us a spirit of timidity, but a spirit of power, of love and of self- discipline. 2 Timothy 1:7

Who of you by worrying can add a single hour to his life? Since you cannot do this very little thing, why do you worry about the rest? Luke 12:25–26

An anxious heart weighs a man down, but a kind word cheers him up. Proverbs 12:25

Cast your cares on the LORD and He will sustain you; He will never let the righteous fall. Psalm 55:22

When anxiety was great within me, your consolation brought joy to my soul. Psalm 94:19

Search me, O God, and know my heart; test me and know my anxious thoughts. See if there is any offensive way in me, and lead me in the way everlasting. Psalm 139:23–24

Therefore I tell you, do not worry about your life, what you will eat; or about your body, what you will wear. Life is more than food and the body more than clothes. Luke 12:22–23

And why do you worry about clothes? See how the lilies of the field grow. They do not labor or spin. Yet I tell you that not even Solomon in all his splendor was dressed like one of these. Matthew 6:28–29

So do not worry, saying "What shall we eat?" or "What shall we drink?" or "What shall we wear?" For the pagans run after all these things, and your heavenly Father knows that you need them. Matthew 6:31–32

A man cannot discover anything about his future. Ecclesiastes 7:14

Therefore do not worry about tomorrow, for tomorrow will worry about itself. Each day has enough trouble of its own. Matthew 6:34

Scriptures on "Depression"

Why are you downcast, O my soul? Why so disturbed within me? Put your hope in God. Psalm 43:5

Find rest, O my soul, in God alone; my hope comes from Him. Psalm 62:5

Anyone who is among the living has hope. Ecclesiastes 9:4

Everything is possible for him who believes. Mark 9:23

The LORD is close to the brokenhearted and saves those who are crushed in spirit. Psalm 34:18

Surely He took up our infirmities and carried our sorrows. Isaiah 53:4

He heals the brokenhearted and binds up their wounds. Psalm 147:3

The LORD upholds all those who fall and lifts up all who are bowed down. Psalm 145:14

The Lord knows how to rescue godly men from trials. 2 Peter 2:9

Scriptures on "Disasters"

Have no fear of sudden disaster or of the ruin that overtakes the wicked, for the LORD will be your confidence and will keep your foot from being snared. Proverbs 3:25–26

I will take refuge in the shadow of your wings until the disaster has passed. Psalm 57:1

In God I trust; I will not be afraid. Psalm 56:4

If the earthly tent we live in is destroyed, we have a building from God, an eternal house in heaven, not built by human hands. 2 Corinthians 5:1

When calamity comes, the wicked are brought down, but even in death the righteous have a refuge. Proverbs 14:32

Then you will call, and the LORD will answer; you will cry for help, and He will say: Here am I. Isaiah 58:9

I call on the LORD in my distress, and he answers me. Psalm 120:1

He brought me out into a spacious place; he rescued me because he delighted in me. Psalm 18:19

Though I walk in the midst of trouble, You preserve my life; You stretch out Your hand against the anger of my foes, with Your right hand You save me. Psalm 138:7

For your name's sake, O LORD, preserve my life; in your righteousness, bring me out of trouble. Psalm 143:11

In this you greatly rejoice, though now for a little while you may have had to suffer grief in all kinds of trials. These have come so that your faith—of greater worth than gold, which perishes even though refined by fire—may be proved genuine and may result in praise, glory and honor when Jesus Christ is revealed. 1 Peter 1:6–7

The LORD will keep you from all harm— he will watch over your life; the LORD will watch over your coming and going both now and forevermore. Psalm 121:7–8

Scriptures on "Doubt"

Stop doubting and believe. John 20:27

Put your finger here; see my hands. Reach out your hand and put it into my side. John 20:27

Be on your guard; stand firm in the faith; be men of courage; be strong. 1 Corinthians 16:13

Remain in me, and I will remain in you. John 15:4

If we are faithless, he will remain faithful, for he cannot disown himself. 2 Timothy 2:13

Now it is God who makes both us and you stand firm in Christ. He anointed us, set his seal of ownership on us, and put his Spirit in our hearts as a deposit, guaranteeing what is to come. 2 Corinthians 1:21–22

The disciples went and woke him, saying, "Master, Master, we're going to drown!" He got up and rebuked the wind and the raging waters; the storm subsided, and all was calm. "Where is your faith?" he asked his disciples. Luke 8:24-25

If you have faith as small as a mustard seed, you can say to this mulberry tree, "Be uprooted and planted in the sea," and it will obey you. Luke 17:6

Have faith in God, Jesus answered. I tell you the truth, if anyone says to this mountain, "Go, throw yourself into the sea," and does not doubt in his heart but believes that what he says will happen, it will be done for him. Mark 11:22–23

I tell you the truth, if you have faith and do not doubt, not only can you do what was done to the fig tree, but also you can say to this mountain, "Go, throw yourself into the sea," and it will be done. Matthew 21:21

See that what you have heard from the beginning remains in you. If it does, you also will remain in the Son and in the Father. I John 2:24

And now, dear children, continue in Him, so that when He appears we may be confident and unashamed before Him at his coming. 1 John 2:28

(C) Resources for Help and Referral

Many times I have found support in people, books, online resources, and audio resources to make a specific, unknown topic become more known to me. I am constantly referring people to others, forwarding their requests for help, making suggestions for additional information and securing permissions to utilize their material, etc. Without these vital links, ministry will not be effective.

Following is a list of sources that I have in my library, that have been not only been a wealth of support for this writing project but also in my assignments as a pastoral counselor and trainer. Some of these may not be in print, but if you are lucky enough to find them in a used bookstore you will be delighted that you have made the purchase.

Resources for further study

A Christian Comfort Companion, Chaplain Maceo Gray, Th. M. and Annie P. Gray, MA Hope Again Ministries Publishing, 2002

A Grief Observed, C.S. Lewis, Seabury Press, 1961

A Sacred Sorrow—Reaching Out to God in the Lost Language of Lament, Michael Card, Nav-Press, 2005

Caring for the Flock—Pastoral Ministry in the Local Congregation, David L. Larsen, Crossway Books, 1991

Companioning the Bereaved, A soulful Guide to Caregivers. Alan D. Wolfelt, PH.D. (Companion Press, 2006)

Experiencing Grief, H. Norman Wright, B & H Publishing Group, 2004

Getting to the Other Side of Grief- Overcoming the Loss of a Spouse, Susan J. Zonneblet-Smeenge, R.N., Ed.D. and Robert C. De Vries, D. Min., Ph.D, Baker Books, 1998

Grieving The Death Of A Friend, Harold Ivan Smith, Augsbury Press, 1996

Guiding People Through Grief—How to Start and Lead Bereavement Support Groups, William G. Hoy, Compass Press, 2007

Healing Your Grieving Heart, 100 Practical Ideas, Alan D. Wolfelt, PH. D. (Companion Press, 2001)

Journey to Joy—In God's Loving Grip Through Two Years of Grief and Loss, Kay E. Thomson, Xulon Press, 2010

Road to Emmaus—Pastoral Care with the Dying and Bereaved, William G. Hoy, Compass Press, 2008

The Grieving Teen—A Guide for Teenagers and Their Friends, Helen Fitzgerald, Fireside Press, 2001

What Does That Mean?—A Dictionary of Death, Dying and Grief Terms for Grieving Children and Those Who Love Them, Harold Ivan Smith and Joy Johnson, Centering Corporation, 2006

When Your People are Grieving, Leading In Times of Loss, Smith, Harold Ivan, Beacon Hill Press of Kansas City, 2001

Where Is God When It Hurts, A comforting, Healing Guide For Coping With hard Times, Yancy, Phillip, Zondervan Press, 1990

Organizations
Alzheimer's Foundation of America
(www.alzfdn.org) The mission of the Alzheimer's Foundation of America (AFA) is to provide optimal care and services to individuals confronting dementia, and to their caregivers and families through member organizations dedicated to improving quality of life.

Cancer Treatment Centers of America (carecenter.com) Cancer Treatment Centers of America® (CTCA) is the home of integrative and compassionate cancer care. They never stop searching for and providing powerful and innovative therapies to heal the whole person, improve quality of life and restore hope.

National Hospice and Palliative Care Association (nhpca.org) This very helpful organization will identify key concepts in hospice and palliative care, locate hospice care agencies in your area, as well as recommend articles and other online reading materials related to death, dying, and bereavement.

Association for Death Education and Counseling (adec.org) The Association for Death Education and Counseling® is an international, professional organization dedicated to promoting excellence and recognizing diversity in death education, care of the dying, grief counseling and research in thanatology. Based on quality research, theory and practice, the association provides information, support and resources to its international, multicultural, multidisciplinary membership and to the public.

Grief's Journey (griefsjourney.com) This website is dedicated to those who have lost a spouse or partner.

Comfort Zone Camps (comfortzone-camps.org) Comfort Zone Camp is a nonprofit 501(c)3 bereavement camp that transforms the lives of children who have experienced the death of a parent, sibling, or primary caregiver. The free camps include confidence building programs and age-based support groups that break the emotional isolation grief often brings. Comfort Zone Camps are offered to children 7-17, and are held year-round across the country.

Eldercare Locator (eldercare.gov) The Eldercare Locator, a public service of the Administration on Aging, U.S. Department of Health and Human Services, is a nationwide service that connects older Americans and their caregivers with information on senior services.

International Society for Traumatic Stress Studies (istss.org) ISTSS is an international, interdisciplinary professional organization that promotes advancement and exchange of knowledge about traumatic stress.

Family Caregiver Alliance (caregiver.org) Family Caregiver Alliance is a national center on caregiving and has services, education programs and publications that are developed with caregivers' expressed needs in mind, to offer real support, essential information, and tools to manage the complex and demanding tasks of caregiving.

The Compassionate Friends (compassionatefriends.org) The mission of The Compassionate Friends: When a child dies, at any age, the family suffers intense pain and may feel hopeless and isolated. The Compassionate Friends provides highly personal comfort, hope, and support to every family experiencing the death of a son or a daughter, a brother or a sister, or a grandchild, and helps others better assist the grieving family.

OTHER RESOURCES FROM PASTOR STEVE

Finding Hope—a children's book about a little girl who loses her smile when her grandmother passes away but finds it in surprising ways.

Finding Hope Grief Activity Book—a coloring and activity book with activities geared toward helping a child who has lost a loved one.

(Coming soon) *The Next 40 Days*—A 40-day devotional through selected Psalms as you journey through disappointments, grief, and other kinds of suffering.

Discover more at www.stevensewell.me.

ABOUT THE AUTHOR

From the small beginnings of being appointed as a youth ministry intern to being a leader in the community, Steve has made it his mission to come alongside others as they encounter loss, change, and adversity. His motivating, positive, and encouraging mentor have made a difference in the lives of individuals, groups, churches, organizations, and businesses, helping them grow to appreciate seasons of change and loss and learn to move forward to reach their goals.

Steve is enthusiastic about life purpose, caring about people, and passionate about values. His heartfelt approach to others is always engaging, never pushy, and always full of open-handed welcome and never fist-pounding demands. He speaks with a wealth of experience from years of his work as a hospice chaplain, bereavement counselor, community/corporate chaplain, pastor, youth worker, author, speaker at conferences and consultant.

Check out these Nonfiction books from
Amazing Things Press

Survival In the Kitchen by Sharon Boyle

Stop Beating the Dead Horse by Julie L. Casey

Fun Activities to Help Little Ones Talk by Kathy Blair

All American Prizefighter by Rob Calloway

Held Captive by Sharon Spiegel

Living in Someone Else's House by David Noe

Overcoming Dyslexia: One Person's Story by Jack R. Newton, Ed.S.

Survival In the Kitchen and Beyond by Sharon Boyle

Menu for a Month by Connie Condron Dow

Easy Recipes from Sandy's Heart by Sandy Smith

Teacher's Tackle Box by Dr. Joyce Piveral, Nancy Piercy, and Sue Nothstine

The Regular Joe: Refills by Jay Kerner

Parenting with Promises by Debbie Kunz

A Century of Service by Roxanne Dale

Amazing Things Press

Made in the USA
San Bernardino, CA
09 February 2020

63932111R00104